MORE ISSUES AT HAND

by the same author*

* James Blish

critical studies in
contemporary
science fiction
by WILLIAM ATHELING, JR.

more
issues at hand

edited
and with an introduction
by
JAMES BLISH

Advent:Publishers, Inc.

Chicago: 1970

to
JOHN BANGSUND
RICHARD BERGERON
RICHARD E. GEIS
and
LELAND SAPIRO

keepers of the flame

Library of Congress Catalog Card Number 72-115400

International Standard Book Number 0-911682-10-4

FIRST EDITION, September 1970
SECOND CLOTH PRINTING, July 1971

Contents

INTRODUCTION:
Criticism—Who Needs It?

ABOUT A DECADE AGO, I WAS A WITNESS IN A legal action, and it became the opposition lawyer's duty to try to destroy my credibility as a witness. One of his first approaches was: "In addition to being a writer, you are also a critic, are you not?" I admitted this, but something even more damaging was to come. He next asked, "Both constructive and destructive, isn't that right?"

I admitted this too, but I shouldn't have done so, for I've since come to realize that there is no such thing as destructive criticism. It is just a cliché people use to signal that their toes have been stepped on.

After all, the whole point of telling a man he is doing

something the wrong way is the hope that next time he will do it right. Simply saying that a given book is bad may serve the secondary function of warning the public away from it, if the public trusts the critic. But if you do not go on to say *in what way* it is bad, your verdict is not destructive criticism, or any other kind of criticism; it is just abuse.

This answers, by implication at least, the question posed by a panel at the Tricon* (1966): Has criticism of science fiction done more harm than good? At least some of the panelists seemed to think that if the critic did not actively love and praise all science fiction, he ought to shut up. This seems to me to be nonsense, though it is a kind of nonsense we hear often in our field.

It is occasioned, usually, by the temporary intrusion into the field of some outside critic—such as the example we saw some years ago in *The Saturday Review of Nothing*—who assumes that because he is ignorant of the field, he is therefore superior to it. I make no brief whatsoever for this kind of critic, but it is a mistake to judge all criticism by its bad examples.

It is also sometimes assumed—as it was by Horace Gold— that even good close criticism scares away new writers, or sufficiently hurts their feelings to impede their production. This may sometimes happen; I have a strong suspicion that I myself scared away one such, but both for his own good and ours he should have been in some other line of work to begin with—especially if his skin was as tender as all that. As for the undeniably good writer who is put off by close criticism, he is probably simply a temporary victim of a remediable condition, namely, his age, which is self-repairing. At his present stage of development he may not be ready for criticism he will welcome later. Since the kind of criticism I am talking about here is a public act and leaves a record behind, he may be able to profit ten years later by what is said about

* 24th World Science Fiction Convention, in Cleveland.

his work now; in the meantime, he may find it very helpful to read what good critics say about the work of other men, where his own feelings are not so intimately involved.

Obviously, then, I think a good critic in any field is a useful citizen, who is positively obliged to be harsh toward bad work. By a good critic, I mean a man with a good ear, a love for his field at its best, and a broad and detailed knowledge of the techniques of that field.

I agree with C. S. Lewis* that the evaluative critic—the man who pronounces on the absolute merits of the work he is considering—is not very useful to either the writer or the reader, although he may be fun to read after you have made up your own mind about the work in question. Some of the more specialized kinds of critic, such as the moral critic, the Marxist and the Freudian, don't seem to be around much any more, and in any event they were never either numerous or influential in science fiction. Where such criticism does flourish, it turns out to be useful and/or illuminating almost exclusively to the writer or reader who shares its basic orientation; if he doesn't, the work strikes him as irrelevant at best. I myself see very little practical use for the historical critic— the man who detects trends and influences, and places individual works in the settings of their times—except to the reader, who might otherwise miss something of what is going on in a work of art by being unfamiliar with the artistic conventions and preoccupations of the work's era. In any event this kind of critical work is tricky in the extreme, and we have nobody in science fiction who does it well (though Leland Sapiro seems to be making a good start at it).

The commonest kind of critic—in science fiction or out of it—is the Spingarnian or impressionist critic. This is the man who believes (though perhaps he has not fully formulated it to himself in just this way) that it's impossible ever to know what the intent of the artist was in writing a given

* *An Experiment in Criticism*, Cambridge University Press, 1961.

work. As a result, he uses the work before him as a spring-board from which to launch a little essay of his own, a new creation which tells you only how he *feels* about the work, nothing about the work itself. At its best this produces something like "On the Knocking at the Gate in *Macbeth*" or "On First Looking Into Chapman's Homer," but there are very few good examples of the breed, and it is plain that their virtues depend upon creativity, not upon critical acumen. Ordinarily, they are nothing but bores—the kind of people who tell you that a spy story was "chilling," or a science-fiction story "mind-wrenching," and nothing more (except, far too often, a plot summary which spoils the book for you). At its worst, it will discuss, say, the New Wave in science fiction by telling you that it is cold in England and rock-and-roll sounds different there.

The technical critic, on the other hand (*not*, please, the scientific or technological one), should be able to say with some precision not only that something went wrong—if it did—but just *how* it went wrong. In writing, as in any other art, there is a medium to be worked in, and there are both adroit and clumsy ways to work with it. Grammar is an obvious example of an area in which a man may be either adroit or an idiot. There are other such areas which are exclusive to fiction, as grammar is not. The writer should know the difference between what is adroit and what is clumsy. If he does not, it is the function of the technical critic to show it to him. Ideally, this work would have been done by the editor, but a surprising number of them don't know how— or perhaps, as Gordon R. Dickson has suggested, they communicate it in private languages which need to be decoded. I would call that a special case of not knowing how, though, for there is a large body of common terms and assumptions in criticism which the editor should be able to use, and the writer to understand.

Such a critic is also useful to the reader. Here his work usually takes the form of *explication du texte*, or what used to be called The New Criticism, twenty years ago. Such a critic uses special knowledge to unearth and expose some element in the work of art which the ordinary reader probably did not know was there. I found my appreciation of the late Cordwainer Smith much heightened, for example, to be told that he was a student of Chinese; such compounds as "ManHome" and "the Up-and-Out" instantly came into perspective for me as ideograms, where each word is also a picture of several different things in combination (mouth + roof = woman, for example). Similarly, a recent analysis of J. G. Ballard in the *Australian Science Fiction Review* went a long way toward accounting for the fragmentary nature of his short stories by showing that despite some deceptive differences in casts of characters, the stories all seem to be part of some much larger story or parable, being seen from different points of view. I might have detected that for myself, but the fact of the matter is, I didn't, and I was grateful to the critic.

This can be useful to the writer, too, by revealing to him underlying themes or preoccupations in his work of which he was not fully aware, and hence enabling him to use them more consciously and hence more effectively if he wishes, or to get away from them if on re-consideration he thinks them becoming obsessive. For examples, see the essay on unconscious symbolism in the second edition of *In Search of Wonder*, or the discussion of the role of syzygy in the work of Sturgeon in *The Issue at Hand*.

The notion that such criticism even *could* do any field harm is a dubious one, and certainly unprovable. Technical critics like Damon Knight are, or should be, invaluable to the writer who is serious about the lifelong task of learning his craft.

And this, I think, answers the question which stands at the head of this Introduction: "Criticism—who needs it?" The answer is, "Everybody."

As an illustration, let me cite the case of Frank Herbert, who is surely one of the finest writers science fiction has today. Yet despite his gifts, his popularity and his awards, Herbert has a major technical fault which is getting in his way: as he tells an already complicated story, he complicates it further by jumping from one point of view to another like a maddened kangaroo. This particular habit doesn't in any way detract from the many things Herbert does marvelously well—but it makes his work more difficult of access for the reader, not out of inherent difficulty, but only because the handling is maladroit. Such viewpoint-shifting has no compensating advantages; it does nothing but show one important aspect of fiction that Herbert hasn't mastered yet.

Maybe it hasn't even occurred to him as a problem. You might be astonished at how many good writers tackle such problems cold, without realizing that they are not the first people in the world to have confronted them, and sometimes solved them. If the critic can point this out, and summarize the solutions other writers have found, he can save the writer time, and also improve the product for the reader.

The case for the critic, in fact, is nothing more than the case for the teacher of any kind: *he saves time*. It was put succinctly by Hippocrates about two thousand years ago: "Art is long, and time is fleeting."

The preceding remarks were first prepared to introduce a panel at the Tricon (upon which, to the possible indignation of Sam Moskowitz, I appeared as Atheling) and later revised for a round-robin for the Science Fiction Writers of America (by whose permission they re-appear here). They stand here in place of a longer essay on the same subject which I published in *Australian Science Fiction Review* in 1967; though the substance of the *ASFR* piece is the same, it was cast as a reply to an *If* editorial by Frederik Pohl and is thus rather less intelligible as an independent piece.

Most of the essays in this book have similar histories. Like their predecessors in *The Issue at Hand* (Advent:Publishers, Chicago, 1964), they appeared for the most part in various science-fiction fan magazines, particularly Larry and Noreen Shaw's *Axe*, Dick and Pat Lupoff's *Xero*, Richard Bergeron's *Warhoon*, Peter Weston's *Speculation*, and in *Science Fiction Times* when it was still under the editorship of James V. Taurasi, Sr.; in *Fantasy & Science Fiction*, a newsstand magazine; and in two professional writers' journals, *Science Fiction Forum* (edited by Damon Knight and Lester del Rey) and *SF Horizons* (edited by Brian Aldiss and Harry Harrison), both now defunct. One was originally a talk given before a fan club at Columbia University; and the opening chapter is drawn from the prefaces to two anthologies of mine, *New Dreams This Morning* (Ballantine, New York, 1966) and *Best S-F Stories of James Blish* (Faber and Faber, London, 1965).

As in the preceding Atheling book, the pieces are arranged roughly by order of first appearance, except where subjects in common among them suggested sub-groups; so whatever continuity the book may have depends chiefly upon an attempted faithfulness to first principles, as stated in the opening chapter of the first book and amplified in the opening chapter (and above) of this one. Also as before, the dates of publication of the originals are given, since the conditions that prevailed at the time of writing of any individual essay do not necessarily prevail now. However, some of the pieces have been revised and expanded from their originals almost beyond recognition, and where that has happened, I have tried to give clear and early warning of the fact in the text. Relatively minor revisions and additions, on the other hand, have been placed within square brackets.

This collection differs from the first one in that a higher proportion of the material consists of book reviews, where *The Issue at Hand* concentrated mainly on magazine science fiction. Addicts of Atheling's unlovably waspish style (there seem to be some) may also detect here a certain moderation of tone, if not an actual softening of the head. This may well be attributable to academicism (in the French sense), marriage, or some other such process, but insofar as it was conscious, it is the result of a gradual conviction that literary and moral flaws deserve to be sharply separated. In his youth, Atheling had a tendency to tear into a bad story as though the author or editor responsible had killed his father and married his mother. This is unfair. While I still believe that it is desirable to be merciless to a bad story, I am no longer quite so sure that the commission of one represents flaws in the author's character or horrid secrets in his ancestry. On the other hand, the authors criticized in this volume will probably find Atheling as offensive as ever, and that is intentional, too.

I am indebted to the editors named above for their hospitality, and to my victims (with one bellowingly enraged exception*) for their patience. I wish I could assure the latter group that William Atheling, Jr. has with this volume reached the end of his tether and wound up his affairs, but it looks now as though he is likely to be around as long as I am. In fact, I have here—as in the first Atheling book—converted into Atheling pieces quite a few that were originally signed,

JAMES BLISH

Harpsden (Henley), Oxon.
1970

---

* Almost exactly four years after the publication of the first book, and two years after the magazine appearance of most of the material about him which is in Chapter II of this one, Sam Moskowitz published a review of the first book which was (among other things) an almost solid mass of factual errors. In the course of this piece he picked up, nearly verbatim, an error of mine which I should like to correct here. In the preface to the first book, I said that "William Atheling" was the pen-name under which Ezra Pound had written music criticism for a Parisian newspaper. It was in fact an English magazine (*The New Age*).

I. SCIENCE FICTION AS A MOVEMENT:
A Tattoo for Needles [1965-66]

WRITERS WHO ATTEMPT TO DEFINE SCIENCE FICtion inevitably suffer the fate decreed by Archibald MacLeish (who was caught by it) for poets who follow armies: their bones are subsequently found under old newspapers. I was reminded of the melancholy fact some years ago when I was set to constructing such a definition for the Grolier Encyclopedia. At that time I could do no better than repeat the usual routine of defining the thing by its trappings—the far journey, the future, extrapolation—but I could not help but feel that when I was done, the emperor had no more clothes than before.

Though I can feel in anticipation the rustling over my bones, I am about to attempt it again, for I've since come to think that the question is a simpler one—O fatal gambit!—

than it is usually made to appear. At least there do seem to me to be certain basic assumptions which stand under inspection, and pass the test by which so many definitions fall: that of remaining applicable to practitioners as apparently incompatible as Ray Bradbury and Hal Clement, yet at the same time clearly excluding the whole category — which everyone *feels* ought to be excluded, however difficult that proves—of fiction about science, as exemplified by *Arrowsmith* or the novels of C. P. Snow. If the assumptions are a little bizarre, I will have to plead that so is the subject-matter; but the argument is reasonably straightforward.

Short stories* of any kind are like tattoos: though they are on public display, they come into being to identify the self to the self. The commonest and hence the most stereotyped were undertaken to prove that the subject/object is grown up, with a flourish of brightly colored but non-functional women, guns, cars and other machinery. Another kind attempts to seal an identification with some stronger and more stable entity—Mother, Mamie, Semper Fidelis or Free Enterprise; or make real some pigeon-hole into which the personality is trying to cram itself—Lover, Killer, Mighty Hunter.

The most interesting kinds, however, are those cryptic symbols which the mentally ill inflict upon themselves. Here the vision of the outside world which the story or tattoo tries to make real is almost as private as the psyche which so stigmatizes itself. Only the necessity to adopt some sort of artistic convention, and to limit the message to something less than the whole of the mystery, makes the end-product even partially intelligible — and, to some part of the audience, holds out the hope that the mystery might be solved.

---

* It is embarrassing to propose a "simple" set of assumptions which cannot proceed two words without running downstairs for a footnote, but I need to add that I am confining myself to short stories for the moment precisely in the interests of simplicity. Otherwise I shall have to ask myself, "What is a novel?" Nevertheless, I think these remarks apply to the science-fiction novel as well, without a great many additional qualifications.

There is at least a little of the private vision in every work of fiction, but it is in fantasy that the distance between the real world—that is, the agreed-upon world, the consensus we call reality—and the private vision becomes marked and disturbing. The science-fiction writer chooses, to symbolize *his* real world, the trappings of science and technology, and in so far as the reader is unfamiliar with these, so will the story seem *outré* to him. It is commonplace for outsiders to ask science-fiction writers, "Where do you get those crazy ideas?" and to regard the habitual readers of science fiction also as rather far off the common ground. Yet it is not really the ideas that are "crazy" but the trappings; not the assumptions, but the scenery. Instead of Main Street—in itself only a symbol—we are given Mars, or the future.

The reason for this choice is put succinctly by Brian Aldiss:*

"I am a surrealist at heart; that is, I'm none too sure whether the reality of the world agrees with its appearance. Only in sf, or near sf, can you express this feeling in words."

Of course, this is not entirely true; neither Kafka nor Beckford had any difficulty in expressing the same feeling in quite different trappings, in sporting quite different tattoos. But for any writer who knows how surrealistic are the assumptions of our modern metaphysics, the science-tattoo is not only attractive but compelling.

It is not even essential that the symbols be used correctly, although most conscientious science-fiction writers try to get them right in order to lure the reader into the necessary suspension of disbelief. There is no such place as Ray Bradbury's Mars—to use the most frequently cited complaint— but his readers have justly brushed the complaint aside,

---

* In *Proceedings of the Institute for Twenty-First Century Studies*, a privately circulated journal of correspondence from science-fiction writers and editors, once edited and published by Prof. Theodore R. Cogswell at Ball State Teachers College, Muncie, Indiana.

recognizing the feeling as authentic even though the facts are not. This is probably what Mr. Aldiss means by "near-sf," as it is what I mean by fantasy. The essential difference lies only in how close to the consensus the writer wants his private tattoo to appear.

In this matter of correctness, the reader also has preferences, so that it is rare to find someone who is drawn to a Hal Clement who relishes Mr. Bradbury too, and vice versa. (For more extended caveats on this subject, please see the penultimate chapter of this book.) However, there are other kinds of accuracy than the factual which are important to poetry (*Dichtung* = any work of art), chief among which is faithfulness to the language of symbol. As precisely this point is pursued at enormous length by Robert Graves in *The White Goddess*, I will rest content with a bare mention of it here.

The absolutely essential honesty, however, must lie where it has to lie in all fiction: honesty to the assumptions, not to the trappings. This brings us back, inevitably, to the often quoted definition by Theodore Sturgeon:*

"A good science-fiction story is a story about human beings, with a human problem, and a human solution, which would not have happened at all without its science content."

This is a laudable and workable rule of thumb, it seems to me, as long as the writer is aware that the "science content" is only another form of tattoo design, differing in detail but not in nature from those adopted by the writers of all other kinds of fiction.

Viewed in this light, the writing of science fiction is an activity which cannot usefully be divorced by the critic from the mainstream of fiction writing, or from artistic creation as a whole. It does not even differ from them in being idiosyncratic in its choice of a symbol-system, since every artist must be odd in this respect, choosing from the real

* First given to the world in a talk before the Little Monsters of America, Caravan Hall, New York, N.Y., 13 July 1952.

world (has anyone seen it lately?) those parts which make the best fit with the universe inside his skull. The science-fiction writer centers his universe-of-discourse in the myths of Twentieth Century metaphysics, as other writers found their intellectual homes and furniture on Olympus or the Mount of Olives.

This feeling of being at home among the apparently wild surmises of modern science is not as rare as it used to be, so that Robert A. Heinlein's conviction that science fiction is *more* realistic than most mainstream fiction—as well as being harder to write—now seems a little dated, especially since scientists themselves have taken to competing with fiction writers in the art of virtually irresponsible speculation. Nevertheless, it is not hard to sympathize with Heinlein, who like Aldous Huxley is impatient with readers who have no contact with the religion of their age, and who like C. P. Snow thinks that the humanist who can tell you who Enobarbus is but has never heard of entropy or DNA cannot fairly be said to be living in the present that surrounds him. Prediction is not the first virtue of science fiction—on this, more later—but Heinlein is surely right in saying that any living man who was surprised by the explosion at Hiroshima would probably have been equally surprised by a head-on collision between two trains previously observed to be speeding toward each other on the same track. Most humanists are *still* stoppering their ears and looking the other way, and hence hardly dare to think that science fiction can be anything more cogent than a Disney fairy tale — amusing now and then, perhaps, but not "real." This kind of behavior is outright stupid; a kinder word for it does not exist.

Nevertheless, the situation *is* changing, as it was bound to do once rockets, nuclear weapons, space travel, DNA and anti-matter invaded the newspapers. Another change—probably a consequence of the news—is that much of the popular fiction the public at large devours today, from *On the Beach* to *Seven Days in May*, is science fiction which has escaped the onus—still anachronistically with us—of the s-f label. Publishers help (though science-fiction fans cannot be blamed for resenting this kind of help) by ducking the label, as they did with Walter M. Miller, Jr.'s *A Canticle for Leibowitz*, or falsifying it, for instance by calling John Christopher's *The Possessors* a "novel of terror" in order to win reviews by detective story reviewers (Anthony Boucher obliged).

On the whole, I think this kind of low-pressure attention better for the field than was the spurious boom of about fifteen years ago, when *Life* magazine was making wildly exaggerated estimates of the number of science-fiction readers, and magazines like *The Saturday Review* were publishing would-be critical articles about science fiction distinguished by nothing but bumptiously complacent ignorance. The process of gradual re-assimilation of science fiction into the mainstream of literature—which was where it started out, with such figures as Wells and Conan Doyle—is bound to be painful for fans who want to claim some special superiority for the genre (as well as for writers who would much prefer *not* to have the usual standards of criticism applied to what they do), but growing up always has its twinges.

The field will *always* remain to some extent a separate, self-conscious branch of letters; that change, which began in 1926, is not in my judgment reversible now. But there is another such change of character now in the making. Science fiction is now in the process of emerging from the status of a small category of commercial fiction, and taking on the characteristics of a literary movement.

It is too early to attempt a history of this change, but some already quite familiar events tend to change proportions and relationships when viewed in this light. Primarily, the change is the work of such magazine editors as John W. Campbell, who whatever his side-hobbies has always insisted that stories written for him have something to say and that the characters in them act and talk like flesh-and-blood human beings, and like Horace L. Gold and Anthony Boucher, who demanded stylistic distinction and who flensed away many of the pulp taboos with which the field was encumbered; of anthologists like William Sloane and Fletcher Pratt, who gave some of the best early stories the relative permanence of book format; of critics like Kingsley Amis and Damon Knight, who saw nothing unreasonable in applying the same standards of judgment to science fiction as are customarily applied to any fiction of serious intentions; and of publishers like Ballantine Books and Faber and Faber, who looked for distinguished work and offered it to the public without either apologies or appeals to special cults of readers. (These citations are intended to be representative, not inclusive, but an inclusive list would not be much longer.)

But the main responsibility for the change, as you would expect, must be assigned to that small but potent group of writers to whom science fiction was not just a meal-ticket but an art form, demanding the broadest vision, the deepest insights, and the best craftsmanship of which each man was capable. The roster of such men is gratifyingly long for its age; and although until recently science fiction has been primarily an American phenomenon, it is gratifyingly international, too. Again, an inclusive list would be impossible without the benefit of greater hindsight than time has yet allowed, but any such list would have to cite Algis Budrys and Theodore Sturgeon in the United States, Brian Aldiss and C. S. Lewis* in England, and Gérard Klein in France. Some of the major editors, anthologists and critics have also contributed as writers.

---

* This citation should raise no eyebrows, but it will. Should anyone ask whether this eminent scholar considered himself a science-fiction writer in any ordinary sense—and a member of the literary fraternity amidst which I place him here—the answer is that he emphatically did. V. the Aldiss-Amis-Lewis discussion transcript in *SF Horizons* No. 1.

What are the characteristics of a literary movement? Everyone will have his own list of distinguishing features—the scholar, for example, will demand that the movement exert some influence on literature as a whole, and this is certainly demonstrable here, all the way from firmly popular writers like Nevil Shute to iconoclasts like William Burroughs—but I think they can all be summed up under the heading of self-consciousness. Among the symptoms of this awareness might be listed the emergence of histories and bibliographies of the field, such as those by Sam Moskowitz and Donald B. Day; of works of criticism such as those by Messrs Amis and Knight (and see the next chapter); of specialized literary quarterlies such as *SF Horizons*, the late international journal edited by Mr. Aldiss and Harry Harrison; of professional organizations such as Science Fiction Writers of America, recently revived by Mr. Knight; and perhaps of such forms of articulate reader support as the "Hugo" and "Nebula" awards (given each year for the best work of the previous year), and publishing houses such as Advent (Chicago) which specialize in works *about* science fiction.

But these remain symptoms. A literary genre cannot also become a movement until a significant number of its primary practitioners, the writers, begin to think of themselves as artists, not just journeymen, working in what to them seems to be the most important and rewarding field of the many they might have chosen. (Note that many of the major science-fiction writers have contributed to other fields as well, particularly the detective story and the historical novel.)

Detecting a writer thinking about himself in this way must remain mostly a matter of reading between the lines. A few —Mr. Heinlein is an example—may come right out and say that science fiction is for them worthy of more attention than anything else being written today, but such statements are often construed as bids for special attention, or pleas for special exemptions from critical attention.*   In any event, most science-fiction writers still tend to shy away from making such public claims.   One place where the claim may be implicit, James Blish has suggested, may be in those stories where they turn to speculating on the future of the arts other than their own.†   Considering how belligerently defensive science-fiction people often are, there is a notable lack of narcissism in these stories; self-conscious though these artists are, they are unprecedentedly more interested in their subjects than they are in themselves.

This freedom from involution among these writers—as contrasted with such authors as Randall Garrett and Fritz Leiber, whose work is filled with and often depends upon inside jokes and even more airless cross-references—may indeed indicate that they are speaking for a movement, of which they are proud.   If that is the case (and necessarily I agree that it is), the movement will have every reason to speak well of them hereafter.

---

* See, for example, the blast against "the Literateurs" (sic) by John W. Campbell in Alva Rogers' *A Requiem for Astounding* (Advent, 1964), p. xix.

† See Blish's collection of such stories, *New Dreams This Morning* (Ballantine, 1966).

II. NEW MAPS AND OLD SAWS:
The Critical Literature [1965]

IT IS THE AUTHORS WHO GIVE SUBSTANCE, shape, and self-consciousness to a literary movement, but it is the critics who define and map it, often give it direction, and sometimes (the proposition is moot) refine it. Together with the bibliographers, the critics also serve to bring the movement to the attention of librarians, a function which is almost never mentioned but is of considerable importance; these three workmen of letters are its conservators and custodians.

As Aldiss and Harrison have pointed out,* it was once widely assumed that science fiction was too tender a plant

---

* Editorial, *SF Horizons*, No. 1.

to be safely subjected to literary criticism. A representative opinion was that voiced by H. L. Gold, who barred critical book reviews from *Galaxy* because he feared that they would scare away authors, particularly new ones. (Gold himself was one of the two most combative editors and editorialists the field has ever seen.)

As Messrs Aldiss and Harrison also note, if there ever was any merit in this notion—which is unlikely—it is thoroughly obsolete now. The man who administered the coup de grâce to it was Damon Knight, who in 1950 began to publish a series of reviews of science-fiction books so uncompromising in tone, and so well grounded in literary experience and taste, as to raise howls about scrub-brushery among the unwashed. (Actually, as Anthony Boucher later observed, Knight's criticism is as notable for its informed appreciation of good work as it is for its savagery toward the slovenly.)

I have discussed Knight's critical work before,* but it is difficult to do justice to it except at length and on its own terms. A fair and extensive sample of it may be found in his book, *In Search of Wonder* (Advent, 1956, 1967). This volume, after a brief but épée-like statement of principles, groups the Knight book reviews by authors and other victims (including editors, anthologies, and a marvelous category called "Chuckleheads"). It is astonishing to see how consistently these assemblages of occasional pieces work out; logic is one of Knight's most attractive traits, buttressed throughout by honesty and wit. The chapters are not ragbags; instead, they constitute studies of most of the major modern science-fiction writers, plus a few long, cold looks at the kind of creaking machine which customarily passes for a classic in this genre.

In Search of Wonder is a useful book for both scholar and practitioner, but its virtues do not end there. In addition, it is so frequently funny, and the engaging personality of its

* *The Issue at Hand*, Chapter 2.

author so unreservedly informs every page of it, that it might well delight readers who have never encountered a line by any of the writers Knight examines. These are much the same qualities which make George Bernard Shaw's music criticism rewarding even for readers with tin ears.

In view of the fact that *In Search of Wonder* is a pioneer work, it is also amazing to see how nearly flawless a performance it is, even this many years after Knight embarked upon the studies it synopsizes. The few cavils I still feel justified in offering are almost embarrassingly minor. For instance, Knight occasionally lets his love of science fiction lead him into confusing large ambitions with dwarf performances, resulting in punchy chapter titles which abuse words like "cosmic," "Parnassus" and "genius," which may please science-fiction fans—who are addicted to hyperbole of this kind—but are not reassuring usages in a critic's hands. There are also some traces of Knight's evolution as a critic, visible mostly in an early tendency to summarize plots in great detail; but these disappear rapidly, nor are they always indefensible—his plot summary of Stanley Mullen's *Kinsmen of the Dragon*, for instance, is perfectly suitable to the preposterousness of its (er, ahem) content, and I can fault it only because I think Knight could have exploded this assemblage of idiocies in less than half the space he devoted to it. (All the same, the review of the Mullen is so funny throughout that I am glad I was never asked where I would cut it). In any event, Knight saw almost immediately that plot summaries are usually imprecise and always clumsy weapons; as the book proceeds, his hand becomes steadily firmer and his instruments sharper. The performance as a whole is outright elegant.

Historically, Knight's criticisms promptly made the mutual-admiration-society or notice-of-availability kind of review look fatuous, and encouraged several other practitioners toward greater severity: in particular, Lester del Rey, Frederik Pohl, Larry Shaw, and even George O. Smith. Some science-fiction reviewers today continue to dispense an almost exclusive diet of stars and kisses, but it is no longer possible to pretend that they do it because they must.

This is not to say that subsequent reviewers in the science-fiction magazines have avoided displaying other slits in the spectrum of ineptitude, such as peddling fan news (P. Schuyler Miller: "I can at last give you some accurate information on the Twenty-third World Science Fiction Convention, which for the second time will be held in London . . ."), diary notes (Judith Merril: "The climate is different here. It rains more. The houses are colder . . . . at four or five in the afternoon, I make a pot of tea . . ."), and self-pity (my favorite example of which, I discover, has been thrown out by my wife, but perhaps that's just as well). These little bursts of self-indulgence, however, are harmful only when they take up a large part of the limited space the magazines can spare for actual reviews of actual works of science fiction. Much more damage is done by fond in-group indulgence informing the reviews themselves. Of these the type-statement might as well be taken from Alfred Bester, since during his brief tenure as *F&SF*'s reviewer he was frequently accused by tender-minded fans of excessive strictness: ". . . it's my policy not to review a downright bad book; I'd rather ignore it than murder it." To this I can only oppose, as an article of faith, my formulation of 1952-3: "To be kind to a bad piece of writing is not a kindness."

My own criticism, as Atheling, of magazine stories—later expanded to include books—was begun in 1952. Though it is considerably indebted to such traditional critics as R. P. Blackmur and Ezra Pound, as one would expect of a writer with a background in such literary quarterlies as *Sewanee Review*, it was most heavily influenced by Knight, with whom I shared schooling in the same literary agency and elsewhere. We had often discussed technical matters, had collaborated on five science-fiction stories and part of a novel, and in

1956, with Judith Merril, founded the Milford (Pennsylvania) Science Fiction Writers' Conference, which Knight has been running with great success ever since, so it is not surprising that we should have many assumptions and preferences in common.

What is surprising is that, with Knight's book and my own, there should still be only five existing volumes of criticism of modern science fiction, even if one counts a book (discussed below) which is primarily historical in intent and utterly naive in what little criticism it does attempt. (I rule out of consideration a hardbound pamphlet by Basil Davenport which, although graceful and charming, bears about the same relation to science-fiction criticism as books on "music appreciation" do to the studies of Sir Donald Francis Tovey). Until lately, under the intellectual pressure exerted by Knight, close and honest criticism simply has not been welcome in this universe of discourse.

Books useful in other ways to the science-fiction writer and student do exist, some of them of considerable interest and including marginal but rewarding critical observations. The earliest of these which still remains worth exploring is a 1947 symposium for beginning writers, *Of Worlds Beyond*, edited by Lloyd Arthur Eshbach.* It contains brief essays (the entire volume, including blank pages and the index, biographical notes and other apparatus, is 104 pages long) by seven long-established writers; their how-to-do-it flavor is well conveyed by their titles. They are: "On the Writing of Speculative Fiction," by Robert A. Heinlein; "Writing a Science Fiction Novel," by "John Taine" (Eric Temple Bell); "The Logic of Fantasy," by Jack Williamson; "Complication in the Science Fiction Story," by A. E. van Vogt; "Humor in Science Fiction," by L. Sprague de Camp: "The Epic of Space," by Edward E. Smith, Ph.D.; and "The Science of Science Fiction Writing," by John W. Campbell.

* Reprinted, 1964, by Advent.

Of these, the best is the Heinlein—a real marvel of compression, every line of which contains good advice for the new writer, but not critical, nor intended to be, except for several buried assumptions about the nature of the idiom itself which Heinlein shares with most other major s-f writers (and some of which he helped to form). (For example, the necessity for honesty toward scientific matters currently accepted as fact.) The van Vogt essay is almost as precise in its recommendations, but because it describes its author's peculiar system of constructing a story by introducing a new idea or plot twist every 800 words (I solemnly swear that I am not making this up), it would be impossible for most beginners to use, and probably pernicious for those few capable of following its advice, van Vogt often included; in any event, what fragmentary criticism is findable in it is all implicit. Taine's piece is solemnly funny about scientific accuracy and how to achieve it; de Camp despite considerable urbanity is no more successful at explaining how to write a funny story than anyone else has ever been; and the other three essays are of no interest now (and probably never were except to the most determined miner of low-grade ore).

A similar but much more detailed and practical volume is de Camp's *Science-Fiction Handbook* (1953). As is the case with most market letters, parts of this book dated very rapidly, but a high proportion of its advice is still good, and much of it would be sound for any beginning writer regardless of his field of specialization. Four chapters of the book's twelve are of critical interest: the first three—about 90 pages—which comprise the best history of the field I have seen; and Chapter Six, which consists of capsule accounts of the careers of eighteen science-fiction writers—Isaac Asimov, Leigh Brackett, Ray Bradbury, Edmond Hamilton, Robert A. Heinlein, Will F. Jenkins ("Murray Leinster"), Henry Kuttner, Fritz Leiber, Frank Belknap Long, C. L. Moore, Eric Frank

Russell, Clifford D. Simak, E. E. Smith, Ph.D.,* George O. Smith, Theodore Sturgeon, A. E. van Vogt, Robert Moore Williams and Jack Williamson. These were probably, as de Camp believes, the most successful science-fiction writers of the period 1926-1950 (to which list one would have to add de Camp himself). The sketches are primarily biographical, but de Camp also strikes off the characteristic preoccupations of each writer incisively, sometimes in a few paragraphs, sometimes in only a sentence or two. (All of these writers except Kuttner, who died in 1958, and E. E. Smith, deceased 1965, are still active, although Long, Moore, G. O. Smith and Williams have appeared infrequently in the past decade, and de Camp, always fundamentally a scholar, has turned to the historical novel.) The *Handbook* is extensively annotated, and includes a fine bibliography—in fact, it includes seven.

I shall mention briefly here Alva Rogers' *A Requiem for Astounding* (Advent, 1964), not because it has any virtues as criticism—Mr. Rogers specifically disavows any such intent—but because it is typical of the kind of book science-fiction fans mistake for criticism, or prefer to read instead of criticism. It is a long (xxiv + 224 pp.) and loving history of the magazine's first thirty years, embellished with many covers and interior illustrations from *ASF*. The text consists chiefly of tables of contents of the magazine, almost issue by issue, plus plot summaries of the stories Mr. Rogers considers most important. The writing itself is enthusiastic, nostalgic and clumsy. Volumes of this kind make up fully three quarters of the existing literature about science fiction. Some, like Donald B. Day's *Index to the Science Fiction Magazines, 1926-1950* (Perri Press, Portland, Ore., 1952), are of obvious bibliographical importance; others, like Mr. Rogers', would

---

* Should the new reader wonder whether any other writers of science fiction have doctorates, the answer is that several do. "Doc" Smith, however, began his career in the days when editors liked to parade any academic distinctions their authors had attained. The custom didn't last, but Smith did. His degree now serves only to distinguish his by-line from that of another E. (for Evelyn) E. Smith.

be of interest only to the most rabid enthusiast. The most astonishing of these "inside" volumes is Sam Moskowitz' *The Immortal Storm*, a history of the publications and internal politics of a small segment of science-fiction fandom, centered upon Mr. Moskowitz himself and written in what appears to be Middle High Neolithic.

Moskowitz is also responsible, however, for one of science fiction's five authentic books of criticism, *Explorers of the Infinite* (World, 1963). (It will be observed that Mr. Moskowitz, like many of his fellow enthusiasts, has a weakness for grandiose titles.) It is a series of biographical sketches of a number of pioneer writers of science fiction, the final one covered being Stanley G. Weinbaum (d. 1936), including summaries of their publishing histories and their plots, and estimates of their influence.

It is this last word which is most important. Though Moskowitz is the nearest thing to a scholar that science fiction has yet produced, his research—as P. Schuyler Miller and others have pointed out—is not always trustworthy; and in the past he has shown an irritating tendency to wax polemical in defense of his errors, in preference to correcting them. Hence, even his most interesting historical and bibliographical discoveries, of which there are a respectable number, are clouded by questions about the primacy of his sources (his account of Cyrano de Bergerac's *Voyage dans la Lune* [1650], for instance, is the work of a man who does not read French), and of whether or not he has really got the facts straight (as he has failed to do in parts of his discussions of Edgar Rice Burroughs and H. G. Wells, neither of them writers whose careers could reasonably be called obscure).

But Moskowitz has chosen his writers in the first place because he believes them to have played important roles in the formation of important traditions, attitudes and assumptions in science fiction, and it is here that his chiefest pretensions as a critic are to be found. Now as anyone who has read much criticism of any kind knows, influence-detecting, though it is one of the commonest of parlor games, is also a very tricky business. It demands common sense, wide reading, a keen ear for language, and enough scholarship to determine whether Author B (the influencee) ever in fact read any of Author A (the putative influencer) and, if he did, what he thought of the experience. Moskowitz is not well equipped in three of these departments, and quite hopeless in the fourth (language).

Let us start with common sense. Though the de Bergerac is often cited in historical summaries (for instance, by de Camp) as one of the earliest of all interplanetary romances, I know of only two science-fiction writers who have read it; one of these is de Camp himself, and the other is Willy Ley, whose contributions to the field include only a few stories. (In one sense, noted above, it could fairly be said that Moskowitz hasn't read it, either.) Hence as a specimen of the primitive interplanetary journey it can be regarded only as a curiosity, neither more nor less influential than such other unread samples as Kepler's *Somnium*—or, for that matter, Voltaire's *Micromegas*. In this light it is especially illuminating to find that Moskowitz completely ignores the late 19th Century utopian novelists; as Miller pointed out in his review, Bellamy's *Looking Backward* and Butler's *Erewhon*, essential to the understanding of Wells' development as to that of many a lesser writer, do not even make Moskowitz's index.

This far from trifling omission may be a failure in the second category, reading. Though Moskowitz may have read more science fiction and fantasy than any other living man— I for one am just as happy to be unable to compete for such a laurel—his knowledge of the rest of literature seems to be a vast blank, flecked here and there by works he has read because their titles misled him into assuming that they were fantasies. As one would expect, this means also that he is unfamiliar with most of the seminal myths of Western culture, which are so fundamental to even the simple enjoyment of fantasy as to make one wonder what on Earth Moskowitz sees in the stuff.

As for an ear for language, Moskowitz has none; a more crucial deficiency for a critic could hardly be imagined. His own style is deadly — pompous, pedantic, humorless and graceless. Some firm editorial hand seems to have removed from this book the solecisms and ghastly grammatical bollixes which are the hallmarks of Moskowitz pure—thus depriving the reader even of a source of unconscious humor— but it remains nevertheless something of a chore simply to get through. As is more evident in his later work—magazine articles on more recent writers—than in this volume, this insensitivity makes it impossible for Moskowitz to detect any sort of influence but that of subject-matter or theme, and that kind of detection is seldom better than guesswork. (For example, he has cited my own "There Shall Be No Darkness" as a direct descendant of Jack Williamson's *Darker Than You Think*; he had no way of knowing—except by asking me— that my story, although first published in 1950, had been written ten years earlier, about eight months before the Williamson was published; but a critic with an ear would have recognized that my story is a schoolboy pastiche of *Dracula*, while the Williamson has quite different ancestors and is at the same time much more original.) A more fundamental objection, however, is voiced with characteristic kindness by Miller:

"It seems to me, too, that the author sees far more imitation—or is it more polite to say 'derivative writing'?— than is fair or just. This may be a matter of experience. Sam Moskowitz is more of a collector/reader and editor than a writer of science fiction. It is commonplace that when the time is ripe, half a dozen writers may start work simultaneously on stories with the same theme or 'gimmick.' At a time when Lowell was lecturing and writing on his belief in an inhabited Mars, it would be practically impossible for adventure novelists not to pick up the hint and set their heroes on the road to the red planet."

Or, more bluntly, this book about the influences which have helped to shape a literature of ideas ignores the effect of climates of opinion.

The fourth of the five critical books we are considering here (the other three being the Atheling, the Knight and the Moskowitz) is less than half the size of *Explorers of the Infinite* and somewhat more limited in its ambitions, but a great deal more successful on virtually every count. This is *The Science Fiction Novel* (Advent, 1959, 1964), which comprises the texts of four University of Chicago guest lectures on science fiction as social criticism. The authors are Alfred Bester, Robert Bloch, Robert A. Heinlein and Cyril Kornbluth, and there is an introduction by Basil Davenport.

It is ordinary enough for the contributions to a symposium to be of uneven merit, but these four essays are uneven in peculiar ways. The poorest is by Alfred Bester, the author of the Hugo-winning *The Demolished Man* and probably the most brilliant (indeed, flamboyant) technician ever to write science fiction. The only idea of substance—and it is pretty wispy—Bester has to offer is a hypothesis that novels achieve popularity and influence primarily as media for the personality of the author. Hence he would have it that his (Bester's) own recent work is better than his rather mechanical pre-World War II fiction because he has in the interim become a nicer fellow.* Nobody who knows him will deny that Alfie Bester is one of the nicest chaps ever to touch ground while walking, but as criticism this essay is a vast disappointment. The hypothesis of course leaves no room for social criticism.

* In a later essay for an anthology which was to contain the favorite short story of each author represented (Robert P. Mills, ed.: *Worlds of Science Fiction*), Bester instead contributed an explanation of why he no longer much cared for anything he had written. It is of course an author's privilege to be diffident, but it is a privilege seldom abused.

C. M. Kornbluth, a superb writer but one much of whose adult career was so submerged in his collaboration with Frederik Pohl that Kingsley Amis (see below) professes to find him invisible, reaches a roughly similar conclusion but upon quite different grounds. Pointing out that such novels as *Uncle Tom's Cabin* and *The Good Soldier Schweik* have catalyzed revolutions, he goes on to the assumption—which at the least would be difficult to disprove—that modern science fiction has had no social *effect*, and then undertakes to ask why. The question was of special interest to him, since the most famous Pohl/Kornbluth novel, *The Space Merchants*, was a virulent attack upon the institution of advertising which was widely read and reviewed by advertising men and many other people not usually exposed to science fiction, is still in print—it has been published in at least one new country every year since it first appeared—and yet quite obviously failed to shake Madison Avenue more than marginally and momentarily. Kornbluth's approach is an examination of this book and a few of its contemporaries, plus such precursors and peers of the socially ambitious s-f novel as *Gulliver's Travels* and Orwell's *1984*, using the instruments of *explication du texte* pioneered in the mainstream by the New Criticism. His conclusion—that modern science fiction goes away from reality, not toward it, and hence is in itself a wish-fulfillment device which does not require the reader to take action in society—is certainly not final, but equally certainly he does not arrive at it out of nowhere.

Robert Bloch's essay is startlingly more interesting than the Bester—startling, because Bloch's own voluminous output of fiction is largely so superficial that he has exerted no visible influence upon any other writer (and at the time of composition of the essay, had not written a science-fiction novel); nor had he been suspected of much critical acumen. The body of the essay is an acid indictment of modern science fiction for its perpetuation of social clichés, especially those of the liberal class. He cites nine major ones, and they make uncomfortable reading. It is Bloch's central thesis that although science fiction mostly does not criticize contemporary society, it should do so; he maintains that the most desirable function of the genre is to shake the readers' assumptions until their teeth rattle. (Amis was later to arrive independently at a similar conclusion.) In Bloch's eyes, therefore, almost the whole corpus of modern science fiction is a spectacle of authors neglecting their duty as social critics. Oddly, he winds up denying this conclusion—or, more specifically, calling the failure he has outlined a criticism of the readers, not the writers—but the point remains, and it pierces.

Heinlein's essay is now moderately well known as the vehicle for his definition of science fiction as a branch of realistic fiction, "much more realistic than is most historical and contemporary-scene fiction and . . . superior to them both." This judgment is highly idiosyncratic, to say the least, and requires more defense than Heinlein gives it; in the essay, it must simply be accepted as a statement of belief. Most of the essay is designed to show science fiction's merit as technological prophecy, a field in which Heinlein himself has been the most successful writer since H. G. Wells, and to document its actual social effects as a spur to real invention. Like Bloch, Heinlein perversely proceeds to deny the point he has just made, but he returns to it promptly in the interests of an even larger, related social claim: that science fiction serves to prepare young people for the technological changes among which they will have to live.

All five of the pieces in the book are well written (though Bloch's style is irritatingly flip), and as a whole the volume is a landmark.

Finally, we have *New Maps of Hell*, by Kingsley Amis (Harcourt, Brace, 1960). This volume is the only existing serious study of science fiction of any weight to have been undertaken by an outsider—that is, by a man who has himself written little or no science fiction (none at that time). It differs from the de Camp, the Knight, the Atheling and the Advent collection in addressing itself primarily to the reader—particularly the prospective reader—rather than the practitioner.

Amis has admitted in person that he knew less about science fiction than he should have when this book was begun, but he is not the complete outsider that some of his reviewers have implied. He has been reading science fiction since about 1934, and his text refers to magazine stories which appeared well before that year (plus, of course, works of Wells and others which were published before he was born). He was for some time a member of the three-man board of selection of the British Science Fiction Book Club, an organization with a considerably better record than its American counterpart (which seems to be a captive creature of Doubleday), and has been the regular science-fiction reviewer, since *New Maps* appeared, for the *Sunday Times* of London. It is perhaps also indicative that his book is dedicated to Bruce Montgomery, widely unrecognized in the U.S. under this, his real name (nom-de-plume: Edmund Crispin), as Britain's leading science-fiction anthologist.

Many of the comments I have seen on the book, however, praise or damn it for quite irrelevant reasons, as well as some that are simply invalid. There has been, for instance, a tendency to laud the book for having wrung from *Time* magazine the first faintly friendly notice ever accorded science fiction as a field by that ill-written and dishonest journal. Why the friendship of *Time* should be considered valuable is beyond me, but in any case it has nothing to do with the merits of the book, which *Time*'s review was incapable of assessing. Writers who are praised by Amis praise him back, in one instance to the point of endorsing a guess of his which is patently untrue; those he damns (or worse, simply ignores) respond with steam-whistle screams. (Hell hath no fury like a woman who can't even find her name in the index.) This is understandable, but again, irrelevant.

The book has many strengths, not the least of which is its wit—as was to have been expected from the author of *Lucky Jim* and *One Fat Englishman*. It is anything but "considerably" arrogant, as its most arrogant critic unluckily alleges; indeed, Amis has no use either for intellectual slummers or for people who see science fiction as the greatest of art-forms, and is at pains to dissociate himself from both types. Furthermore, as noted above, he is aware of the existence of gaps in his knowledge, if not always of their extent, and admits them readily. No more can I see why opinions which have been in formation over a period of 26 years should be labelled "ill-considered"; the book is in fact extremely reflective in cast, no matter how many of its conclusions one may disagree with.

The same critic alleges "unconsidering slovenliness of research," which is nonsense, and leads me to the suspicion that the three accusations involved are not so much the product of critical judgment as of the game being played with the verb "to consider." There are, to be sure, some errors, and some omissions, but they are quite minor. On page 46, for instance, Amis is unable to remember the title or author of Hal K. Wells' 1932 story, "The Cavern of the Shining Ones," hardly a crucial lapse; and he spoils Sprague de Camp's anecdote at the top of page 60 by making its protagonist a science-fiction writer instead of a *Weird Tales* writer, thereby missing an interesting but altogether minor psychiatric point (horror stories often have a strong sexual appeal; science fiction, almost none, as Amis himself later notes). In general, it is quite plain that Amis has read far more science fiction than most of his critics. He is also immensely better read in traditional fiction, which gives him a great advantage over people with only one string to their bows, but not, it must be added, an unfair one. For documentation see the index, which by the way is excellent.*

The book has also been criticized—for once, relevantly—for its marked bias toward the *Galaxy* type of story. This is in part a product of the author's personal taste, about which nothing can be done; but in part, too, many of those doing the complaining have only themselves to blame. In the course of preparing the lectures at Princeton which resulted in the book, Amis sent extended questionnaires to many writers and editors in the field; and report has it that the returns came largely from the Pohl-Gold/Ballantine axis, thereby heavily skewing the data for which Amis was searching.

This is nevertheless a real weakness, however it came about. What seems to appeal most to Amis in science fiction is social satire, so much so that he readily swallows a great deal of such work ranging from the pathetically inept to the downright awful. It is this bias that leads him to his now notorious deification of Frederik Pohl (and perhaps to his weird parallel assumption that in the Pohl-Kornbluth collaborations, Pohl did the thinking and Kornbluth stuck in the action), which I suspect is already an embarrassment to both men and is likely to become more so as time goes on. Of greater consequence than overestimating an individual writer, however—for on such a matter there is often no possibility of honest agreement between one critic and another—is the encouragement this bias lends to further proliferation of social satire in science fiction, a sub-class which had reduced itself to a cliché and a bore some time before Amis came on the scene to give it his endorsement. I at least would maintain that rather than calling for better examples of the type, as Amis does, what we should ask for is a moratorium on the damn thing. It has already been done very well, middling well, not well at all, and absolutely miserably, *ad nauseam*; and its subsidiary, in

---

* The Ballantine paperback edition of the book abridges the index, but pays for this in part by adding a feature of great value: a list of all the stories and novels mentioned by Amis which were then available in paperback editions.

which science fiction satirizes itself, has become a positive blight on the landscape.

Personal taste, skewed data or both also bias the book toward the one-punch type of story, of which the work of Robert Sheckley is properly singled out as the best example. This bias, unlike the previous one, is surprising in a sophisticated science-fiction reader, simply because such a reader is almost impossible to surprise. It is characteristic of a Sheckley story, as it is of the work of less polished writers of the same kind, that the punch can be seen coming some pages ahead of the moment when the author delivers it; and if the punch is all the story has—as is almost invariably the case— nothing remains but Sheckley's incidental wit (or in lesser writers of the same kind, nothing at all).*

I would further disagree with Amis' contention, on his page 101, that satire on individual persons and corporations is universally absent in science fiction. I'll not resist the temptation to point out that my own *They Shall Have Stars* (first published in England) devotes about a third of its wordage to a personal attack on the late Sen. McCarthy, a point U.S. McCarthyites—as my mail showed—were quick to recognize. McCarthy indeed was quite a favorite target of American science fiction, as was only to have been expected; for instance see Kornbluth's *Takeoff* or Richard Condon's more recent *The Manchurian Candidate.* Corporations? Well, the higher echelons of General Electric were in no doubt whose ox was being gored in Kurt Vonnegut's *Player Piano*, as I know from having worked for one of their public relations agencies that year, and this book we can be sure Amis has read (see his page 149). Nor was a drug company that I worked for in any doubt about who was being satirized in my own *The Frozen Year*, which appeared in England as *Fallen Star* with an Amis jacket endorsement. (In fact, they nearly fired me.) I would not go so far as to maintain that this kind

---

* This point is discussed at greater length in *The Issue at Hand.*

of satire is a common feature of science fiction, but it's there. Whether or not we need more of it is another question.

A particularly interesting aspect of Amis' book is his personal approach to the history of the genre. He rejects the claims for antiquity of the field made by most of its historians—such as the attempts by de Camp and Moskowitz, among others, to capture Lucian of Samosata as an ancestor —maintaining instead that modern science fiction is a peculiarly Twentieth-Century phenomenon, with earlier roots in Wells *et al.* but becoming significant only with the advent of the American specialized magazines in 1926. I do not think he makes a very good case for this, for it seems to me that it is impossible to understand much of what is going on in modern science fiction, particularly among the satirists whom Mr. Amis so much admires, without at least some reference to the Nineteenth-Century utopians; but his view has at least the merit of limiting his universe of discourse to what is characteristic of science fiction as it is practiced now. It is probably true that in this universe, "the marvelous voyages" of antiquity have very little significance, except to fans in search of respectability.

Despite these various dissents, however, *New Maps of Hell* was a job that badly needed to be done, and for the most part has been done wondrous well.

Afterword: 1968

Shortly after the appearance of this essay, a new volume by Sam Moskowitz appeared (*Seekers of Tomorrow*, World, 1966), which I subsequently reviewed both for *Amazing Stories* and an Italian magazine, *Nova SF** (Bologna; the asterisk is not a footnote sign, but a part of the title). At last reports the Italian version had yet to appear; and since the *Amazing Stories* version had to be confined to a very small space, what follows is an amalgamation and revision of the two.

In addition, four other books of critical and bibliographical importance deserve notice.

The Moskowitz book (which also appeared in paperback from Ballantine Books in 1967) picks up where its predecessor left off. It includes sketches of 22 science-fiction writers: E. E. Smith, Ph.D., John W. Campbell, Murray Leinster, Edmond Hamilton, Jack Williamson, "Superman," John Wyndham, Eric Frank Russell, L. Sprague de Camp, Lester del Rey, Robert A. Heinlein, A. E. van Vogt, Theodore Sturgeon, Isaac Asimov, Clifford D. Simak, Fritz Leiber, C. L. Moore, Henry Kuttner, Robert Bloch, Ray Bradbury, Arthur C. Clarke and Philip José Farmer. There is also a chapter called "Starburst" dealing briefly with a number of other writers, an Introduction and an Epilogue.

This volume further illuminates Moskowitz's two methods of detecting an "influence," both of them highly unscholarly. In the first place, since he cannot detect stylistic influences, the resemblance he finds between a given story and its successor(s) is almost always the superficial one of a common idea or gimmick. Even in a genre which places as much of a premium upon new ideas as does science fiction, such ideas are rare and grow increasingly so every year. Since at least about 1938, treatment has become steadily more important than springboard notion. Science-fiction writers borrow such notions from each other freely, to an extent that in other fields would sometimes be indistinguishable from plagiarism; this is almost never resented as long as direct quotation is avoided, and the resulting story is commonly welcomed as fresh if the borrowing writer succeeds in looking at the old idea in a new light—whether that light be dramatic, emotional, or even simply technological. Innovations of *this* kind, which are far more important in any literary field than any single germinal notion, are what make or break modern science fiction.

This Moskowitz method and its complement can both be seen at work in two sentences from this book (pp. 366-7): "Judith Merril, who established her reputation with "That Only Mother,"* a story of a mother who can see nothing wrong with her mutated, limbless child, published in *Astounding Science Fiction* for June, 1948, certainly owes some inspiration to Bradbury, whose touching vignette, "The Shape of Things," in *Thrilling Wonder Stories* for February, 1948, deals with a woman who can see nothing wrong in her child, born in the shape of a triangle. James Blish, who went on to win a Hugo in 1959 with *A Case of Conscience*, a novel of the dilemma of a priest on a planet where creatures exist without original sin, should bow respectfully in the direction of Bradbury's "In This Sign" ("The Fire Balloons"), published originally in *Imagination*, April, 1951, which tells of priests who go to Mars and discover Martians without original sin."

It can be seen from this quotation that once Moskowitz has spotted what he thinks to be the first appearance in print of a fantasy premise (in the case of the Bradbury-Blish example, he missed it by about 350 years, an unusually wide miss but otherwise not untypical), he assumes that all subsequent appearances of the idea derive from that first story— not only regardless of its merit, but in the face of frequent physical impossibility. In making these judgments he is governed entirely by publication dates; no record exists of his ever having asked any living writer when a given story was first written (though in science fiction, where almost all of the writers he considers important are either still alive or were at the time he was writing about them, this would have been uniquely easy to do).

In the Merril-Bradbury example above, for instance, he

---

* The title of this story, which is far and away Miss Merril's best known, is: ". . . That Only a Mother . . ." Moskowitz's mistaken version of it is alas all too typical of both his accuracy and his proofreading—and every one of these bloopers is faithfully reproduced in the paperback edition.

apparently simply does not know that the lead-time between
the mere acceptance of a story and its publication (unless, in
some rare cases, the story is very short) is almost never less
than a year—without even taking into account the time the
author had to spend (a) in writing it, and (b) in sending it
around to its possible markets. Inquiry to Judith Merril
would have revealed that the story of hers in question was
written in the spring of 1947, as she has testified (*F&SF*,
Sept. 1966, p. 22)—and as a matter of fact I myself saw the
manuscript at that time. I have already noted the impossibility of the Williamson-Blish "influence" Moskowitz detects
on p. 97. Moskowitz in fact has been known to defend,
noisily, a publication gap between two stories of *less than
one month* as being significant of priority (see Knight's *In
Search of Wonder*, second edition, p. 133).

In addition, in making these dubious points, Moskowitz
is not above stretching the pertinent dates to make his case
seem more credible. For instance, above he cites the original
publication of "The Fire Balloons" in the April, 1951 issue
of *Imagination*, a widely unread magazine then in its fourth
issue; whereas he makes it appear that *A Case of Conscience*
was published in 1959 (by citing the date of the novel version's Hugo award, given for the best novel of the preceding
year). He knows very well (because he says so, on p. 412)
that the first half of the novel—containing, intact, the idea
he cites—appeared in the September 1953 issue of *If*, six
years prior to the date Moskowitz is trying to pass off in the
quotation above. If this is not dishonest, it is at least dis-
ingenuous. For whatever the author's testimony is worth,
again, my Agreement with Twayne Publishers, Inc., the original contractors, shows that the novelette version of "A Case
of Conscience" had been delivered to Twayne by February
1953. Prior to that time the manuscript had been read by
three magazine editors (Horace Gold, Lester del Rey and
Larry Shaw), moving the date of its actual composition well

back into 1952. It certainly cannot have been influenced by anything I saw in *Imagination*, a magazine then known to me only as the boneyard for one of my first and worst stories.

That this is bad criticism is obvious; but the ignorance of publishing mechanics it betrays also suggests again that Moskowitz's reputation for reliability in matters of fact — the main ground, or last ditch, at which his work is usually defended—may be somewhat overblown.

The new book is also full of typos and misspellings. For example, in discussing my own "Cities in Flight" series, the text has both "okies" and "Oakies" for "Okies," and "spin-dizzy's" for "spindizzies," a complete strike-out. (Incidentally, Moskowitz says on p. 76 that this four-volume novel "may well have" been inspired by an Edmond Hamilton serial published when I was eight years old, nearly two years before I had even seen my first science-fiction magazine. Again, the facts are that I didn't know of the existence of the Hamilton story until Robert W. Lowndes mentioned it to me circa 1952, and I haven't read it to this day. Harry Harrison tells me that Moskowitz is dead wrong about the "inspiration" of his novel *Deathworld*—which Moskowitz also misspells. And so on. Examples such as these lead me to the suspicion that whenever Moskowitz says "certainly" or "may well have," it is a warning that he is talking through his hat.)*

During this same period, a new professional science-fiction writer named Alexei Panshin began to publish, in fan magazines both in the United States and overseas, a thorough and perceptive full-length critical and biographical study of Robert A. Heinlein, which was subsequently published, after considerable revision, by Advent (1968) in book form. This

---

* In all fairness, the reader should be warned here that very late in 1967, well after all of the preceding material was written and most of it was published, Moskowitz published in a fan magazine a major attack upon my practice as Atheling. I report this for the record.

is the best single-author study of a recent writer ever to be published in our field, in my opinion.

Inasmuch as I was asked to write an introduction for the book version, and did so, I shall not go further into detail here; my opinions are in the front of Mr. Panshin's book, and what little inducement they may add to your buying a copy I am not about to subtract by repeating myself in my own book. I do want it to be thoroughly understood, however, that this Panshin work is criticism of the highest order, and belongs in any list of the few truly critical works science fiction can boast.

The attention of librarians, and of anyone else interested in bibliographies, should be called to the MIT Science Fiction Society's *Index to the S-F Magazines, 1951-1965* (Cambridge, 1966; compiled by Erwin S. Strauss), a valuable and enormously thorough continuation of the Day *Index* mentioned earlier in this chapter. Equally valuable is *The Index of Science Fiction Magazines, 1951–1965* (El Cerrito, Calif., 1968; compiled by Norm Metcalf). Fans of Brian W. Aldiss, of whom happily there are a great many (though not yet enough), should also acquire *Item Forty-Three*, a complete bibliography of his work from 1954 to 1962 by Margaret Manson (Dryden Press, Birmingham, England, 1962).

III. THINGS STILL TO COME:

Gadgetry and Prediction [1964]

IN A RECENT SYMPOSIUM,* LESTER DEL REY
has contended that much current science
fiction is living in the past, or at least in
the present; that we as writers are still preoccupied with
space travel and atomic energy, though these were among
science fiction's first gadgets and are now realities. Both del
Rey and Frederik Pohl made the point that writers ought
now to be thinking more about such subjects as molecular
biology—a point that wrings vigorous nods from me, since in
my "pantropy" series† and elsewhere I have been pounding
that beat since about 1942, mostly without any company.

* "SF Since the Atom Bomb," *Epilogue*, Vol. I, No. 2, 1964.
† James Blish: *The Seedling Stars*. Gnome Press, 1956; Signet, 1959, 1964.

In thinking the matter over, however, I attempted to run a brief tally of how much science-fiction gadgetry has actually become reality, and how much remains unrealized and still worth playing with. Two things about this second list—which was rather cursory, since it came from memory alone—surprised me:

1) The list is rather long. Many of the dominant gadgets of science fiction are still not with us, and indeed some of the most popular ones do not seem to be even close to technological realization yet.

2) Some of these notions, which used to be common fare in science fiction, have now almost disappeared from the stories. This fact, of course, immediately made me wonder why it should be so.

The simplest and most obvious of these once-favorite devices is the field drive or anti-gravity, and as a sort of subspecies of it, the energy screen. I lump these two things together despite certain conceptual differences because they were most often used in stories for similar purposes: lifting a ship or some other mass without benefit of rockets, propellers, or any other form of prime mover which might be noisy, heavy, or require large amounts of open space for its safe operation. In all the old stories, it was remarkable how quietly and neatly spaceships lifted off, or indeed how unobtrusively a robot butler might float into a room, clean up the breakfast table or deliver a message, and then float out again. Floating on what? The author seldom said, but the convention itself is one of long standing.

Well: where is there so decorous a prime mover? Nowhere in sight in the real world yet. As long as relativity remains the fundamental world-view of physics, anti-gravity is decreed to be an absolute impossibility. There are, to be sure, a number of large laboratories, not all of them surrounded by secrecy, where gravity research is now going on, and where several suggestive discoveries are emerging. It is now rather generally agreed, for example, that gravity is propagated as a wave, though its behavior is by no means so simple as the waves we are familiar with in electromagnetic phenomena. And there are a number of bold spirits, even at this late date, still trying to shoot holes in poor old Einstein, though their successes still remain to be achieved. There is some hope—some minimal hope—that anti-gravity may be still in the offing, but I think it will be a safe subject for science-fictional games for decades to come.

And there are doubtless still new things to be done with it. There was a certain amount of incredulity, not to say consternation, when in my "Okie" stories* I picked up whole cities and flew them off into space, but after all, if one has a true anti-gravity drive, there should be no limit to the size of an object one can lift with it, and there is no visible reason why it has to have an aerodynamic shape; it is not going to be travelling at aerodynamic speeds while it is in an atmosphere, and streamlines are unnecessary in space. Thus even a little simple thinking about an apparently outworn gadget can be found to yield unexpectedly broad conclusions.

As for those energy screens, the child in me still cherishes the moments in the E. E. Smith epics when layer after layer of fiercely attacked screens would radiate into the ultraviolet and go down under the ravening rays of the Fenachrone or the Chlorans. But when is one of those screens going to go *up*—not layer after layer of them, but just one?

Though Smith's discussion of the theory of such screens was limited to some magical talk about different orders of energy (none of which turned out to have any counterparts in the real physical world), it is clear that he thought of them as stationary wave fronts. They resemble what might happen if the light of a star, after proceeding in the usual expanding-bubble fashion for a certain distance, were suddenly to stop

---

* James Blish: *Cities in Flight* (series). Faber & Faber, London, 1965; Avon, 1967.

dead at that distance and refuse to allow outside light of identical frequencies to pass.

Well, this is not wholly unreasonable. Waves out of step do cancel each other, and waves in step reinforce each other (to the eventual overloading of their generators); and if one kept such a screen continuously supplied with power as it was cancelled out by the opposing vibrations, it might be kept in existence for some useful length of time. The question is: How does one stop a wave-front in its tracks? Insofar as I can see, one doesn't; but there are dodges by which an equivalent effect might be achieved. Such effects are often seen in waveguides and in other phenomena of that general field, which is called resonance, and to achieve them in free space one needs only to create a resonance effect without a resonator.* Or, one might turn to current gravity theory and to an effect called the Standing Wave, about which Poul Anderson has written at some length. The point is, these screens are still there to be exploited, and they are not going to come into reality very soon.

From screens, it's a natural step to rays, the great happy hunting ground of the old-time science-fiction writer, and the staple of space opera. Writers in those days imagined their readers to be tireless in demanding, "Where are the gadgets?"; and there was a sort of open competition among us to come up with ever newer and more outlandish ones. This was nowhere more apparent than in the field of weaponry, and particularly, in sidearms. This day is so long gone that most readers now are probably strangers to that rich spectrum of lethality which the readers of the 1930's could revel in; the modern writer must be content with dispatching the villain with that standard piece of imaginery hardware, the blaster. Well, we didn't scorn the blaster as a tool in the thirties, but

---

* I have no idea how this might be done, though I made some guesses in a story called "The Box" (Blish: *Galactic Cluster*, Signet, 1959); but part of the fun of these questions is that they are still wide open.

it was strictly a brute-force weapon, more suitable for bulling through doors and walls than for killing, and I think most of us felt—more or less instinctively—that anything with a name like that probably was too bulky a machine to be toted for normal personal defense. E. E. Smith's semi-portable projector pretty well exemplifies how we thought of the blaster.

No, our side-arms were subtler. We had rays that would kill you by coagulating your proteins, as though you were a hard-boiling egg. We had rays that would carry a deadly electrical shock, of course—that was beginner's stuff—and poison rays which would turn your blood into furniture polish. We had several different types of disintegrator, which either made you vanish completely or turned you into fine dust or pocket-flug; about the only thing they had in common with each other was that they seemed to take quite a few seconds to do the job, which would be a serious defect in a real side-arm. Edmond Hamilton, having heard that matter is really energy and that waves out of step cancel each other, invented a heterodyning ray which blanked you out like an unwanted radio program; the victim disappeared with a loud bang, while the gun itself only hummed decorously like an Atwater-Kent loudspeaker.* We had rays which would drive you insane; rays which would throw you into convulsions; rays which would paralyze you; rays which would melt you down like a tallow candle. Harl Vincent invented one which covered you with hundreds of buzzing, spinning little black discs, which wore you rapidly down to nothing but a curl of greasy smoke; the wicked temptress in the story† carried this in her index finger, a notion I am glad Freud died before encountering. And of course we had heat rays, from Wells onward; and Ray Cummings had a cold ray, too.

Where are they now? Silent in Gaza. A decade or so after John W. Campbell declared the heat ray to be a permanent

* "Monsters of Mars," *Astounding Stories*, April 1931.
† "The Copper-Clad World," *Astounding Stories*, September 1931.

impossibility, we have the laser gun, which is a heat ray. It can set fire to your clothing, or blind you at a fair distance, or, if your skin is bare, can make you reach for the Unguentine. Presumably more ferocious models will come later. And radar will cook you like an egg, too, if you stand too close to a high-powered antenna, but the effect is too short-range to be useful. Nothing else remotely resembling the death rays of old is around now, and furthermore, nobody seems to be writing about them now. Why not? They were lots of fun, and since nobody seems likely to invent one in the real world for some time to come, there's still plenty of room for ingenuity. And rays are just the beginning. One of my own favorite inventions is the kangaroo shiv, an apparently ornamental dagger worn by the ladies, which has an explosive charge embedded at the base of the blade. If the lady can't stab you at close range while you are besieging her virtue, she can pot you with the blade from clear across the room—but if she misses, of course, she's deliciously defenseless, and the pirates are even now pouring through the airlock....

Where are the tractor and pressor beams of yesteryear? They have yet to appear in the real world and there is no theory upon which any such thing could actually be designed; yet they have also disappeared from science fiction, handy though they undeniably were.

And what ever happened to free flight? By that I mean flight without a surrounding machine; or with a bare minimum of a machine, like the flying belt. This is one of the oldest of science-fiction dreams, and although there are some beginnings at realizing it in the real world, fully-controlled, long-range free flight is still a dream. But who is dreaming it? It seems to have vanished from science fiction more than a decade ago.

Invisibility is another subject which used to be standard fare in science fiction and which has now itself vanished. Did it go away just because it was played out? I'm inclined to doubt that; I suspect that it was simply the victim of a fashion. To be invisible, like being able to fly without a machine, is one of the great wish-fulfillment dreams, and so should be an almost inexhaustible subject for a writer. H. G. Wells did a brilliant job of showing the disadvantages of invisibility—indeed, all of his early science fiction is cautionary in tone, as indeed it was bound to be in view of the fact that it was deliberately modeled on Dean Swift—but what of its joys? Is there nobody left in the world with just a little of the Peeping Tom in him?

I sometimes think that if there is any truth in the tired allegation that science fiction has lost its sense of wonder, it may reside in the fact that much modern science fiction has lost its childishness—and I mean childishness not in its innocence, but in its sinister and amoral sides. For example: when I was just going into adolescence, one of my favorite daydreams was one in which I would suddenly arrive over the Earth in a mile-long spaceship, which would become a permanent fixture of the skies and from which I would rule all the world as invincible overlord, proving to the teachers who had failed me and the girls who had scorned me that I was a person of substance after all (but by then it'd be too late). I suspect that this is a fairly common fantasy; it has many features in common, at least, with the adolescent suicide fantasy which has been so often reported. What interests me now about it is that, although I became a writer of fantasies, I never did put that particular one on paper; so that when, decades later, Arthur C. Clarke did,* I wound up kicking myself vigorously for having wasted what was all too obviously a powerful, almost mythical notion, one which could not fail to move the kind of reader who likes fantasy at all. [But see "Skysign," *Analog*, May 1968, which placed last in the readers' choice.]

The invisibility fantasy is another such notion. I think

* *Childhood's End*. Ballantine Books, 1953. N.B. Mr. Clarke's title.

an important part of Mr. Clarke's success as a fiction writer (I exclude his achievements as a popularizer of science and of science-fiction prophecies, which is an entirely different kind of skill) can be attributed to the use—the unashamed use— he made of these semi-erotic, semi-irresponsible daydreams, which he told as soberly as though they were as worth taking seriously as hard truths. Instead of clinging to them in privacy, shame, or penuriousness, he voiced them for all of us, as though he were reporting an important part of the real world. And of course he was; hence, how could we have failed to be moved?

In a famous story with a long number for a title, Alfred Bester convincingly showed that at least six of the great standard science-fiction notions—The One Man Who Can Save the Earth, The Last Man on Earth, and so on—are in fact erotic daydreams of a peculiarly retarded sort, and that one of the functions of this sort of writing may be to purge us of them. In so doing, he went back, effectively, to the cautionary tale of Wells; he showed us, for instance, that being the last man alive in a world of women would emphatically not be a position we would really enjoy. These points were worth making and were spectacularly put; but they are the morals drawn by a completely mature adult who looks upon the auto-erotic element in science fiction with some contempt, and, I might add, a certain modicum of Puritanism which would probably quite surprise him.

But daydreams do have functions of their own, of which the purgative is only one and—*pace* Aristotle—not necessarily the most important. They also speak for the gratifications which we really hope to find in life, no matter how crudely they may limit, simplify or otherwise falsify them. Certainly the race as a whole cannot get away from them as a class, no matter how many individuals manage to outgrow this one or that one. All children dream of flying—all male children, anyhow—and of being changelings; they all like guns and have visions of power, omniscience, irresponsibility, potency, grandeur. As Eric Hoffer has pointed out, among adults the weak subsist on almost nothing else, and it is in the long run from the weak that the actual realizations of some of these visions spring—the genuinely powerful are too comfortable to rock the boat, and they can obtain elsewhere the gratifications for which the weak must imagine feats of enormous ambition and daring, and then bring them to pass.

Science fiction has always spoken for these daydreams. Today, most of the magic is being worked by psionics rather than by rays and invisibility, but this again is just a matter of fashion—generated, I suspect, by the writer's desire to appear plausible. He knows he can't justify death rays or anti-gravity or invisibility—so he turns to something nobody is even going to ask him to justify. But along with this taste goes the tradition of the cautionary tale, which has its place but cannot be put into the service of a daydream because it turns it sour. As an example, consider the Asimov story which points out that the advent of a time-viewer—not a time-travelling machine, but just a viewer—would automatically abolish privacy, because such a machine would not care whether it looked a million years into the past, or just one second. A frightening thought as Asimov handled it, because he took an adult view of it; but a Heinlein would have used the same brilliant insight to bring out the Peeping Tom in us (what *did* happen to the spy rays of yesteryear, by the way?), and I suspect we'd have liked the resulting story rather better. Much of Heinlein's work is devoted to precisely this exploitation of our most fundamental, most anti-social childishnesses, and I know nobody who doesn't love him for it no matter what we think of his McKinleyesque politics. Much of Lester del Rey's power, back in the days when he was producing most of his major work, derived from the same source.

I do not want anyone to think that I am decrying the cautionary tale. Most of what we label as "mature" science fiction takes this form, of which the anti-utopia is only one aspect. Poisoning wells is a legitimate function of the writer, and I have done so myself occasionally with considerable glee. It might be noted, too, that when Wells' science fiction turned from the cautionary to the visionary, it lost a good half of its impact.

But I venture to suggest that lately it has been somewhat overdone; I at least would just as soon not read another anti-utopia for some time to come, much though I've admired several ventures in that form. There is more to science fiction than just making more new maps of hell. There is still something to be said for wish-fulfillment, too, and I suspect that any modern writer who adopts this strategy — given, of course, the necessary minimum of skill — will cut a wide swath through what is at present a somewhat bored audience.

It is even possible that this is the road back to that ambiguous sense of wonder.

IV. FIRST PERSON SINGULAR:

Heinlein, Son of Heinlein [1957]

IT IS NOW SOMEWHAT LATE TO REMEMBER that the novel was not always the major vehicle of science fiction; but s-f novels were scarce before World War II. Up to that time, the magazine story thoroughly dominated the field.

One of the first writers to make this transition was Robert A. Heinlein, who until his war-time disappearance from the magazines had been a commanding figure among the remarkably many and remarkably exuberant writers who made the 1940's so explosive and influential a period in the development of science fiction. Many magazines were put down the drain by the wartime paper shortage, and Heinlein himself went into war work; when he returned, he chose to refurbish his career as a writer of books.

He has been fabulously successful at it, and one reason for that success has been the high grade of machinery which goes, today as always, into his story-telling. Heinlein seems to have known from the beginning, as if instinctively, technical lessons about fiction which other writers must learn the hard way (or often enough, never learn). He does not always operate the machinery to the best advantage, but he always seems to be aware of it.

I don't mean to imply, by the way, that this is the sole source of Heinlein's strength as a writer. It is simply that aspect of his writing which I want to talk about here; insofar as I can manage, the focus of all these essays is technical.

One of these technical lessons is that of the unified point of view. This discovery—that the continuity of a story and its feeling of unity is improved if it is told throughout from the point of view of a single character, usually the protagonist—is only about a century old,* and though it is a particularly powerful device in the short story, some of the world's greatest short stories (especially the Russian) make no use of it. Nevertheless common practice has awarded it a triumph; other ways of "seeing" a story range now only from rare to obsolete, and it is outright mandatory in commercial fiction.

Heinlein's use of this device was once generally remarkable only for its irreverence—in, for instance, the way he dropped out of the point-of-view for one or two thousand words of straight lecture whenever he pleased. In the novel form, however, Heinlein has shown a special interest in the most difficult of all points of view: the first person story, told by the principal actor. Among the adult novels he has handled in this way are *The Puppet Masters*, *Double Star*, and *The Door Into Summer*. [For five more recent—and rather special—cases in point, see the Afterword to this essay.]

* It is usually credited to Flaubert.

First person is the most difficult of all masks for the writer to assume, because it is the most difficult *persona* to keep separate from that of the writer himself. A skilled writer does not adopt it arbitrarily, but for good technical reasons (for instance, it is virtually obligatory when the point-of-view character does not know that he is the hero, as in *Double Star*), and he is under the same obligation to make the first-person narrator real as he would be to make a third-person viewpoint-character real. To the unskilled writer, on the other hand, first person is a trap. It becomes an exercise in autobiography; that constantly recurring word "I" irresistibly leads the writer back into himself, and away from the kind of narrator the story being told needs.*

Heinlein is a highly skilled writer, but by instinct†—and he has now caught himself in this trap three out of four times. Twice he has bailed himself out by dazzling virtuosity in handling other aspects of the story. The third novel, however, proved to be so closely tied in substance to the problem of viewpoint that its failure to solve the problem killed the story.

The failures of masters are usually more interesting to the technician than the triumphs of tyros, and this one is no exception. The only first-person narrator Heinlein has created who is a living, completely independent human being is The Great Lorenzo of *Double Star*. Lorenzo is complete all the

---

* Another common trap of first person singular is what might be called "retrospective inconsistency." It is found in novels wherein the narrator has undergone a more or less drastic change of heart by the time the book ends—yet the beginning of the story, supposedly being told by the man who has already undergone this enlightenment, shows his state of mind firmly entrenched in its former attitudes. I don't recall that Heinlein ever made this mistake, but some examples may be found in *The Space Merchants* (C. M. Kornbluth and Frederik Pohl), *Preferred Risk* ("Edson McCann"—Pohl and Lester del Rey) and my own *The Frozen Year*. Two of these books won prizes.

† Untrue. At the time I wrote this, I had not seen his contribution to the symposium *Of Worlds Beyond* (see pp. 22-23 above), which shows him to be thoroughly conscious of technical problems *per se*.

way back to his childhood—the influence of his father upon what he thinks is one of the strongest motives in the story—and his growth under pressure is consistent with his character and no-one else's. On the other hand, the heroes of "Gulf,"* *The Puppet Masters*, and *The Door Into Summer* are all the same man: the competent young engineer-operative, sentimentally hard after the model of the fictional private eye, politically conservative, contemptuous of the ordinary man, philosophically wedded about equally to "common sense" and the doctrine of Progress, fast-talking, wise-cracking, and quick with his fists. By drawing on all three novels, a critic could produce quite an extended portrait of this man, but in no one of the novels is he presented in the round; and I think it is quite safe† to assume that he is in actuality an idealized self-portrait of the author. On the few occasions when Heinlein has spoken for himself in print [in autobiographical notes and convention speeches], he has offered opinions and attitudes completely coherent with those of his triple hero—which I offer not in proof but simply as additional documentation; the appearance of the same hero in three independent novels should be proof enough.

In *The Door Into Summer* Heinlein has apparently come to take this hero so for granted that he does not even try to set him forth clearly for the reader—a defect which is fatal to the novel. Presented with the task of showing us not one, but two future societies, Heinlein bungles both because he has failed to visualize precisely *who* is seeing what there is to be seen. Dan Davis has so little personality of his own that there is hardly anything in the world of 2000 A.D. in which

* Not a first-person story, but very firmly a part of this canon.

† It wasn't safe at all; Heinlein reportedly was furious. I sympathize, for ordinarily the temptation to identify a first-person character with the author is one the critic ought to resist. Nevertheless, this author's subsequent development—and particularly, the more and more naked political and philosophical editorializing in his recent work—convinces me that this is a special case, and one which defies understanding except in these terms.

he can legitimately be interested. He has no interests beyond robots, revenge and his own financial affairs, and so when he looks around at 2000 A.D. he sees nothing but a few abstractions [and a few highly perfunctory details, such as the amazing things—unspecified—the ladies can do with a new kind of dress material]. The major feature that comes through is not Dan Davis at all, but pure Heinlein without even a false beard: this is the attack upon the parity system of farm price supports, which is applied in 2000 A.D. to automobiles. Though the subject is something of a sitting duck—I have yet to encounter anybody who will defend the parity system — the attack is marvelously funny and well done, but it in no way emerges from anything we have previously learned about Dan Davis' interests. (It is surely an odd novel that is at its *best* when the author is openly editorializing.)

What about the novel's heavy emphasis upon cat protocol? This, surely, is characterization? No, not in any major sense. Davis' affection for Petronius the (sic) Arbiter, and the elaborate pains he takes toward securing the animal's well-being, form a part of the broad stripe of sentimentality that lies just beneath the hardness of Heinlein's triple portrait, and they do help to make the portrait more believable; an exaggerated regard for animals is a common trait in people who are unusually callous toward human beings, and Davis' obsession with Pete adds credibility to the heroine's betrayal of him. But in *The Door Into Summer*, the hero's love for his cat is little more than a funny hat that he wears; were Dan Davis to speak with a stutter, or collect postmarks, the effect upon the structure of the novel would be about the same. (I don't deny that it would deprive the novel of its title gimmick, but this would not be a major loss.) Most importantly, there is nothing to be seen in the world of 2000 A.D. for which the cat protocol is illuminating.

Unless my memory has failed me, *The Door Into Summer* is Heinlein's only major essay in time travel, and as such it should have been a major novel.* Every other important subject of science fiction which Heinlein has examined at length has come out remade, vitalized and made the author's own property. It didn't happen here, for the first time in Heinlein's long and distinguished career—and not because Heinlein didn't have something to say, but because he failed to embody it in a real protagonist.

Evidently, Heinlein as his own hero is about played out.

Afterword: 1967

Since the above essay was written, Heinlein has published six more first-person novels: *Time for the Stars, Have Spacesuit—Will Travel, Starship Troopers, Glory Road, Podkayne of Mars*, and *The Moon Is a Harsh Mistress*. None of these uses the Dan Davis kind of hero. All but *Glory Road* and *The Moon Is a Harsh Mistress* are teen-age novels; *Glory Road* is a sword-and-sorcery fantasy, with a heavy overlay of casual sex, apparently Heinlein's most recent fictional discovery. The viewpoint character of *Podkayne of Mars* is a loathsomely precocious teen-age girl; like the heroine of Heinlein's *Saturday Evening Post*-type story "The Menace From Earth," Podkayne is snappish, stupid, self-righteous and dull—an unsuccessful attempt to turn the ordinary, eminently slapworthy suburban chick of the 20th Century United States into a vehicle for interplanetary romance. *Have Spacesuit—Will Travel* is, as its title suggests, a sort of pilot script for a

---

* At the time of writing I was reminded by my editors, Damon Knight and Lester del Rey, that "Heinlein's long novelette, 'By His Bootstraps,' must be considered a major essay in time travel in its effect, if not its length." Possibly; but this story, plus " 'All You Zombies—,' " a later effort, is not much more than an exploitation of the circular paradox. Neither story contains more than one character—in fact, neither would exist if it did, since each specifically sets out to make the viewpoint character the *total* population of its universe. This kind of thing makes a fine stunt, but characterization is irrelevant to it.

dead-on-arrival television script, which is used as a vehicle to preach Heinlein's doctrine that man is a highly dangerous wild animal. (This, as Poul Anderson has pointed out,* is a wholly romantic notion; it seems truer to the facts to hold, as Anderson does, that man was far and away the first of all animals to be domesticated.) Similarly, *Starship Troopers* —though as pure narrative it is an exciting piece of blood and thunder—is heavily burdened with an attempt to demonstrate that the military veteran is of all adults the most responsible man politically, in flat defiance of the historical evidence; it also makes a brief pitch for Dr. Edward Teller's contention that a little fall-out is good for you. This one is also extraneously interesting for the light shed on it by *Glory Road*, whose hero is a combat veteran with about as much political responsibility as a mink. *Glory Road* itself, however, is devoted chiefly to an equally irresponsible sexual relativism (though a very mild one, confined strictly to standard heterosexuality; Heinlein's heros turn their backs, blustering, upon any form of deviant behavior like a he-man accosted in a washroom). The narrator of *The Moon Is a Harsh Mistress* is not its hero at all; the computer is.

What is most interesting for my purposes about all the recent novels, however—not just those in the first person— is that in them the editorializing has become blatant (sometimes, as in *Farnham's Freehold*, to the near-extinction of the story), so that it is no longer necessary to apply any sort of detective work to the problem of what Heinlein thinks; he tells you, and at length. In particular, the political conservatism of Dan Davis and his twins has intensified into a reactionary radicalism indistinguishable, except for the intelligence with which it is defended, from the positions of the John Birch Society and the Minutemen. In short, it is no longer possible to pretend that Dan Davis' attitudes are those of a *persona* adopted solely for literary purposes.

* In *S-F Forum* No. 1.

Heinlein is already unique in science-fiction history in many important respects, and his political development further sets him off from his fellow practitioners. From H. G. Wells on, the main current of social thought in science fiction has been liberal, even, despite some preoccupation with the Superman, egalitarian—so thoroughly that, as Kingsley Amis complains, many of the liberal assumptions have gone underground and become clichés, to the frequent impediment of both logic and imagination. Thus even Heinlein's worst recent novels (especially *Farnham's Freehold*) exert a shock effect all out of proportion to the dwindling amount of craftsmanship that has gone into them.

It seems unlikely, however, that this aspect of Heinlein's *curriculum vitae* will have anything like the influence upon his peers that his previous innovations did. "The gulf between us," as a Heinlein superman remarks,* "is narrow but it is deep."

---

* Appropriately, in "Gulf."

V. DEATH AND THE BELOVED:

Algis Budrys
and the Great Theme [1961]

FROM HIS FIRST MAGAZINE APPEARANCE IN science fiction, Algis Budrys was clearly a born writer, as opposed to the technicians who have lately dominated this field. Budrys is, inarguably, a technician himself, and a consummately skillful one, but his gifts go far beyond craftsmanship into that instinctual realm where dwell the genuine ear for the melos and the polyphony of the English language, and the fundamental insight into the human heart.

I do not in the least mean to disparage craftsmanship. It is essential, and that realization is what made the science fiction of the 1940's so strikingly, gratifyingly superior to most of what had been published before. It is the reason why new-comers like Heinlein, Kuttner, and del Rey were able effort-lessly to push offstage writers who had dominated the genre for many years, and furthermore, keep them offstage while other newcomers with respect for their craft filled in the lower echelons. Budrys is among other things a late but per-fect example of this kind of craftsman—and in addition, a stunning example of how greatly such a man can enrich En-glish from a grounding in an almost totally unrelated language (in Budrys' case, Lithuanian).* Indeed, were science fiction not so tiny and easily ignored an enclave of English letters, I think Budrys would by now be known as the finest writer in our language as a *second* language since Conrad and Nabokov. Technique can hardly take a man farther than this, wherein-ever he chooses to work.

Yet it is striking that there has been no qualitative change in magazine science fiction since the technical appreciation of the 1940's, even if one counts some fairly striking changes in subject-matter. The technicians-per-se are still front and cen-ter, and the newcomers to their ranks have acquired the firm notion that a bag of tricks—a rather small bag—is all there is to writing (or at least, all that's needful to keep selling). The next logical stage, the infusion of genuine human emo-tion into the speciality, has by and large failed to materialize; we have no writers who are consistently trying to write sci-ence fiction the hard way.

There are of course writers who have tried it now and then —"Stuart," del Rey, Kornbluth, Sturgeon, Bradbury, and perhaps one or two others—but successful though they

* Budrys' full name is Algirdas Jonas Budrys, which in Lithuanian means "Gordon John Sentry." He was born in 1931 in what was then Koenigsberg, East Prussia. His father was Consul General of Lithuania, first in Germany, and then in New York City, until his death in 1964. The elder Budrys' primary duty after the sovietization of Lithuania in 1939 was to maintain a climate in which the U.S. would continue to support the pre-war regime's diplomatic missions. Ayjay was his translator, speechwriter and assistant between 1939 and 1960.

sometimes were in bringing it off, they failed to set an example the majority of science-fiction writers were willing to follow. Any number of reasons could be adduced for this, and I will offer here only the most immediately obvious:

(1) Individual writers such as Bradbury and Sturgeon proved to be too idiosyncratic for other writers to follow without turning into disciples or outright parasites, especially since they made their understanding of English a form of private property;

(2) Striving for genuine human emotion is one hell of a lot harder work than mastering a Mysto Magic Kit, especially at two or three cents a word; and,

(3) The overwhelming majority of science-fiction readers have made it clear that they actively distrust and dislike emotional content in stories, even in the rare instances where the author has it under perfect control. (Admittedly I would find this last point difficult to demonstrate, but I think the list of Hugo winners—especially when compared with their defeated competitors—strongly suggests it, for a starter.)

These are not the only factors involved, but they alone are enough to cripple the writer who wants to produce this kind of text. They have duly crippled four of the five examples I have named; the fifth, who was never entirely at home here anyhow, had the good sense, both artistic and financial, to get out. They have never crippled Budrys in any visible way; and although he too appears to be on the way out, he has left us *Rogue Moon* (Gold Medal, 1960), as a testament and a promise.

The novel (the version published by *F&SF* is about as representative of the whole as a veal cutlet is of a calf) is a testament to the fact that Budrys the science-fiction writer is the only one of his generation who has never stopped growing and learning. (In fact he is almost the only one to show himself capable of learning anything at all, so we are phenomenally lucky that he did it on so grand a scale.) That he had many good gifts was evident from the outset, but in addition he has prosecuted their use to the uttermost limits of his strength. If he is now to go on to a larger audience, as he should, it is only after writing a work which epitomizes everything he has ever had to offer us.

So it is no surprise that *Rogue Moon* is a masterpiece. It would have been visibly a masterpiece in any year; it was especially conspicuous in 1960, a year in which its nearest competitor (and that was not very near) was an admittedly electrifying blood-and-thunder novel — Harry Harrison's *Deathworld*—harking back (even in its uncertain grammar) to the dear dead days of Harl Vincent and Charles Willard Diffin. No other entry showed even this much merit, though several were ambitious enough in intent.*

A full-scale analysis of *Rogue Moon* might turn out to be nearly as extended as Stuart Gilbert's study of *Ulysses*, so I am not going to attempt it here. Though the plot is deceptively simple, both conception and execution are so complex that such an analysis would be scanty were it twice as long as the novel itself. Nor would I have the brass to offer the "essence" of the case, which is knowable only to Budrys. But in my own universe, two layers of this multiple structure bulk largest.

As I read this book, then, *Rogue Moon* is primarily a man-against-nature story in which the devices, the symbols, the machinery being brought to bear upon it by the author are those of modern warfare. The battlefield is the death machine on the Moon; the weapons are the technology mustered to get through the machine, logistics included—which, with

---

* The Hugo winner for that year was *A Canticle for Leibowitz*, by Walter M. Miller, Jr., a superb novel and a landmark in its own right. I had no intention of slighting it in these comments, but I was persuaded at the time—and am still, for all the difference it makes now—that it should have won the award the previous year and was not eligible for 1960. The committee made it eligible on a technicality. It certainly deserved a Hugo, but it is sad that it had to nose out *Rogue Moon* to get it.

marvelous appropriateness, are as deadly as the death machine itself, killing "us" even before "they" do, *but without our being aware of it*. This point is driven home by the device of the duplicated man, who although he dies many times both on Earth and in the death machine and is able to remember each death, can never be convinced that he is not the same person who began the experiment.

There are two stories being told: the apparently simple man-against-nature yarn, and the pacifist parable. It is also clear, however, that the "nature" of the first story and the "enemy" of the second are identical, and that neither of them are located on the Moon; they are in the souls of the men themselves, in short they are not "them" but "us." After all, the death machine (like any other fact of nature) has been there for a million years without killing a soul, and it is far from certain—indeed, highly unlikely—that killing men is what it was designed to do. The two-fold enemy is the viewpoint character's drive for knowledge at any cost, and that of the secondary lead for suicide. In this case, much is made of the military value (potential, because wholly unknown) of the death machine; hence, knowledge-is-power, and there you have the two sides of modern warfare in one coin: lust for power on the one, suicidal mania on the other.*

If I am making it sound as though both male leads in this story were crazy, I have understated my case. The entire cast of characters, including all the minor ones, is as various a pack of gravely deteriorated psychotics as has ever graced an asylum. I cannot remember ever encountering before a novel in which all the characters were demonstrably, clinically, incurably insane, including the hero and the heroine, but that is the fact here. Nor is it inadvertent; not a word in this book is.

* Budrys, a student of politics, has disavowed any specific pacifist point; he describes the book as an "open" novel, capable by intention of bodying forth any of several consistent interpretations. But this might be said of any work of art.

Why did Budrys populate his book solely with madmen? For two immediately visible reasons. One is embodied in the book's epigraph, a motto off a tombstone by which the author plainly says that he considers the situation in the book quite normal — at least for our times. In other words, he means *you*, and me, and himself. The other is to be found in three pages of an imaginary Arthuriad, in tone rather reminiscent of the historical romances of Maurice Hewlett but a good deal more distinguished, in which the leading character is compared to Merlin fashioning invincible armor for Lancelot, whom he hates. This, plainly, is the pacifist parable again, applying not only to the bombsmiths and others who are accumulating the means for our forthcoming suicide, but to all the rest of us who acquiesce in it. The motive given, both for the hero and for Merlin, is pride.

(The author's preferred titles for the book, by the way, were *Halt, Passenger* — from the epigraph — and *The Armiger* — from the imaginary play. [He would also have settled for *The Death Machine*.] Hence I doubt that I am laying greater stress on these two elements than they were intended to bear. *Rogue Moon* was the publisher's title, which, as Budrys has remarked, suggests that the novel is about a riverboat gambler.)

There are two love stories involved, one concerning the hero and his girl, the other involving the secondary lead, *his* girl, and a truly loathesome villain who is distinguished both by being the most pitiable character in the book, and by being no crazier than anybody else in it.* This quadrangle is, of course, actually a sort of serial orgy, by virtue of the fact that every time the secondary lead comes home he is all unawares a different man; and the simpler love story is actually a triangle for the same reason, though the hero *is*

---

* Several readers of this review objected that they did not find the villain "loathesome." My view of him was perhaps colored by the fact that I worked for nearly a decade for exactly such a man. In any event, I am inclined to agree that when one flings adjectives like this about carelessly, one is left with none to describe such characters as Goneril.

aware of that and his awareness gives Budrys a tremendous curtain-line.

Virginia Kidd has noted that the two concepts of love embodied in these relationships are both markedly immature. The secondary lead's girl is almost a prototype of the all-devouring adventuress, la belle dame sans merci, the vulva-with-teeth; the hero's girl, on the other hand, is his mother. I find this perfectly in keeping; what *would* have startled me would have been finding anyone in this cast of bedlamites depicted as capable of a mature love relationship; but Budrys has better sense than that.

Then there is the question of what eventually happens to the man who dies many deaths. The author has so cunningly constructed his ambiguity here that you may finish the book perfectly convinced that you have been told plainly what finally happened to that man. Look again. The fate that you—not the author—have awarded this character may tell you a good deal about yourself, though the chances are excellent that you'd rather not have known.

All this material is so close to the surface that it may seem glaringly obvious to Budrys, and an act of usurpation for a reviewer to lay it out so simplistically. On the other hand, there is a good chance that some other layer of meaning may have bulked much larger to the author; at least I have said enough, I think, to show that this seemingly straight-forward piece of yarn-spinning is in fact marvelously complex. There are some areas of the novel, furthermore, where I can see the complexity but I don't know what it's for. For instance, the horrifying passage through the death machine which takes place toward the close of the story is not only a tour de force of inventiveness, but has also been put together to suggest that each menacing situation or death presented by the machine has its counterpart in an episode of the story proper. I can see this but I don't know what to make of it; is it perhaps only a piece of virtuosity to delight the author, like

Joyce's cramming the names of more than three hundred rivers into *Anna Livia Plurabelle* because the chapter was about a river? Since in this case the relationship between the sequence of events in the machine and the sequence of events in the story is structural, it must be doing more work than this, especially since it is strongly underscored that neither character in the machine sees what the other sees—a situation which applies to each reader vis-à-vis the book as a whole (as is true of any work of art) . . . .

And this line of reasoning leads so directly to the point that I'm amazed that it ever baffled me. The passage through the death machine is structurally analogous to the book as a whole because Budrys, through the motive he assigns for going through the machine at all, wants to comment on the reason why a man troubles himself to produce a work of art: *To do something nobody has ever done before.* The book abounds in such philosophical points, equally tightly integrated into its action.

As a testament, *Rogue Moon* is more than impressive; it is not only a bequest but a monument. As a promise, it is more nebulous because no author can make promises for himself, let alone for any other writer. Nevertheless I think it shows once more that a science-fiction novel can be a fully realized work of art, provided that it comes from the hands of a dedicated artist who also knows the field, and who is neither frustrated by the patent indifference of his audience nor handcuffed and hobbled by an obsessive subject. Budrys is not the first man to do this, but you will not need more than one hand to tick off his peers; he is leaving science fiction from the top step.*

---

* Five years later, after a turn as an editor of a major slick magazine, Budrys returned to writing. In a letter in mid-1965, he said: "I wish I could come back into the field with something strange and marvelous to show for my absence, but I believe I will merely come up with something strange . . . But I would not be mumbling so gloomily if I didn't feel optimistic." At the age of thirty-four, he— and his readers—have every good reason for optimism.

VI. CAVIAR AND KISSES:

The Many Loves of
Theodore Sturgeon [1961]

THE SUBSTANCE OF THE ESSAY WHICH FOL-
lows was originally written as an appreciation, for the special Sturgeon issue of
F&SF celebrating that author's appearance as the Guest of
Honor at the 20th World Science Fiction Convention in Chicago, 1962. In that version it was wholly laudatory; as I told
Ted even before its publication, I also had some reservations
about his work, but did not think it appropriate to include
such sour notes in what was after all supposed to be a festival
overture. He was aware of some of these reservations, since
I had touched upon them before in print;* and I think it is

* See *The Issue at Hand*.

now appropriate to expand upon them here. As will be
readily apparent, they dim my admiration for his writing
only very faintly indeed.

One of the minor mysteries of Theodore Sturgeon's macro-
cosm is his hostility* toward a popular and thoroughly competent story called "Microcosmic God." If you compliment
the author on this yarn, he is likely to respond with the polite
purr which is as close as he can usually come to a snarl. If
you don't mention the subject, Sturgeon will probably bring
it up himself.

It's a good story; why the antipathy? I don't propose to
try to read the author's mind, which I regard as one of the
major critical crimes; but looking back at "Microcosmic God"
(1941) over the landscape of Sturgeon's long career, one can
see that it is an atypical Sturgeon story in a number of ways.
One of these differences lies in its central character, Kidder,
who is—let us whisper it—a scientist maddened by power.

It's unlike any other story about a mad scientist you are
ever likely to encounter, but its theme is about as close as
Sturgeon has ever come to being conventional. It is characteristic of much of other writers' science fiction that its central figures tend to be great scientists, senators, galactic presi-
dents, space-fleet admirals, interplanetary spies, and other
wheelers-and-dealers, though very few of the authors involved
have ever met so grand a man as their state assemblyman or
even know his name. Sturgeon's work is not like this.

Sturgeon's characters, if assembled in one room, would
make a marvelously motley crowd, but almost all of them
would be people you would not look at twice in any crowd
—not even if you knew who they were. A few bulldozer
operators; a little girl disowned by her family (but how could
you tell that?); a male clerk; a ragged outcast; a boarding-

---

* N.B. to printer: That word is "hostility," *not* "hospitality" as it unhappily
appeared in *F&SF*.

house peeping-Tom (but how would you know?); and so on. Ordinary, all of them—with the almost unique exceptions of Kidder, the mad scientist, and the anti-hero of "Mr. Costello, Hero," who bodies forth almost blindingly the author's positive and pure loathing for all wheelers-and-dealers.

This is not to say that any of these people is in the least ordinary in Sturgeon's hands. A good many of them are what most readers would regard as rather repellent characters, but Sturgeon almost always handles them with the love—not the forgiveness, which is another matter entirely—that is born of understanding.

This is, I repeat, a rare quality in science fiction, and of course a valuable one. And it leads us to another and even more important fact about Sturgeon's work: It is intensely personal.

Most writers who cling to some one form of specialized fiction—whether it be the detective story, the Western, or the slick story—do so, I have often suspected, because these more or less stereotyped forms do not require them to reveal themselves. As a good many other people have observed, any serious work of fiction is bound to be autobiographical at least in part. It was Thomas Wolfe who said that it would be hard to imagine a more autobiographical work than *Gulliver's Travels*—a startling choice of example at first encounter, but the more one mulls it over, the more just it seems. Category fiction requires no such tapping of the inner life. Science fiction in particular has often been criticized for its conventionality, and even more for the cold, cerebral atmosphere which its authors seem to prefer to breathe. Though these authors have as many idiosyncrasies of style as a porcupine has quills (unlike most reliable producers in other standard categories), the *emotional* tones of what they produce are virtually interchangeable.

Sturgeon's work is charged with highly personal emotion —so much so that it seems to embarrass his younger readers, who like science fiction precisely because it puts little stress on their own untried emotions. (And here it might be added that the emotional tone of "Microcosmic God" is pretty standard stuff for science fiction—which again makes it highly atypical Sturgeon.)

Kingsley Amis and others have also pointed to the undoubted fact that there is very little sex of any kind in most science fiction, and this fits nicely with my hypothesis that science-fiction authors cling to the genre because it doesn't require them to reveal themselves. For any author, writing about sex is at the beginning a hard hump (not "lump," please, printer) to get over, because it will reveal (or he thinks it will) a knowledge of matters previously supposed to be not proper, or perhaps even positively forbidden, depending upon his upbringing. That very first sex scene is almost impossible to write if what is really on your mind is, "Suppose Mom should read it?" I have the undocumentable suspicion that many science-fiction writers, including some of the major ones, have never gotten beyond this point in their development, and don't want to, either.

All of Sturgeon's major work is about love, sexual love emphatically included. He has so testified, but had he kept mum about the matter it would have been discovered anyhow; it is right there on the page. This, for Sturgeon, is far from a limited subject, for he has stretched the word to include nearly every imaginable form of human relationship. Here again I think he is probably always in danger of embarrassing a large part—the juveniles—of his audience; the rest of us are fortunate that, if he is aware of this danger, he evidently doesn't give a damn.

This is, as he himself has said, why he has written so much about complicated biological relationships involving three or more partners, most of which have technical names hard to find even in good unabridged dictionaries (e.g., syzygy, which doesn't appear even in Roland Wilbur Brown's magnificent

Composition of Scientific Words). It is why, in recent years particularly, he has seemed so preoccupied with telepathy; it has nothing to do with the didactic madness on this subject which has dominated so much of the field (thanks mostly to John W. Campbell) since World War II, but instead reflects his larger preoccupation with all the possible forms of love relationships, even the most peculiar.* It is significantly different from the kind of telepathy one usually finds in such stories, too; in fact, what Sturgeon seems to be talking about is not telepathy at all, but something I am tempted to call telempathy—a barbarous word, but perhaps no worse a one than its model. Sturgeon's word for it is love, and a very good word it is.

Directly under this heading belongs Sturgeon's love affair with the English language, which has been as complicated, stormy and rewarding as any affair he has ever written about. He is a born experimenter, capable of the most outrageous excesses in search of precision and poetry; people who do not like puns, for example, are likely to find much Sturgeon text almost as offensive as late Joyce (and I am sorry for them). Nobody else in our microcosm could possibly have produced such a stylistic explosion as "To Here and the Easel," a novella based in language as well as in theme on Ariosto's 16th-Century epic *Orlando Furioso*, because in fact nobody else would have seen that the subject couldn't have been handled any other way. (L. Sprague de Camp's and Fletcher Pratt's *The Castle of Iron* is also based on Ariosto, of course, but solely with comic intent and effect; the Sturgeon work, despite considerable lightness of touch and even some jokes, is primarily intensely serious.) And even Sturgeon's verbal excesses are his own; he does not call upon exotic or obsolete

---

* Of sexual perversions, a subject most science-fiction writers stonily pretend doesn't exist, Sturgeon has remarked: "It is fashionable to overlook the fact that old-shoe lovers *love* loving old shoes." Dante would have understood this perfectly, only going on to add that *simultaneously* they also hate and fear it.

words for their own sakes, or otherwise the multitudinous seas incarnadine; he never says anything is ineffable or unspeakable, the very ideas embodied in those words being foreign to his artistic credo; he does not splash color on with a mop, or use the same colors for everything; and he does not say "partly rugose and partly squamose" when he means "partly rough and partly scaly."

This quality of freshness of language even when it is out of control—which is not often—is due primarily to the fact that Sturgeon is an intensely visual writer. His images come almost exclusively from what he sees, as Joyce's came almost exclusively from what he heard. (Sturgeon is a musician, as Joyce was, but his various attempts to *describe* music and its effects are all failures, reading at their worst like the kind of copy found on the jacket backs of jazz LP's.) Readers who do not think in terms of visual images—a very large group, as the electroencephalographers have shown us; perhaps as many as half of us—are likely to be baffled by this, or at least put off. They will get along much better with a writer like Poul Anderson, who follows a deliberate policy of appealing to at least three senses in every scene. Sturgeon's extremes of visualization probably lie at the root of the rather common complaint that he is a "mannered" writer.

The charge as stated is untrue, for Sturgeon has many manners, adopted or cast off at the bidding of the subject-matter—in comparison, for instance, to a writer like Ray Bradbury, whose gestures and locutions seldom vary from work to work. But it is true that Sturgeon is often to be caught in visual similes that must seem wild indeed to that body of readers whose minds work most comfortably with abstractions. One of the commonest of such complaints in my experience homes on his comparison (in *More Than Human*, one of the very few authentic masterpieces science fiction can boast) of marmalade with a stained-glass window. Most of the complainers call this simile "strained" (in itself an un-visual word to apply to anything having to do with marmalade); yet to me it seems as just as it is startling, in particular when one observes that the man in the book to whom this breakfast is being served, and to whom the comparison occurs, is actually trembling on the verge of starvation.

It is possible—though I hope it is untrue—that Sturgeon's almost lifelong concentration upon the ramifications and implications of a single subject has reached the point of diminishing returns, like Heinlein's exploitation of the first person. Objectively it can at least be seen that his once considerable production has fallen off sharply; this is only emphasized by his 1964 Pyramid collection, *Sturgeon in Orbit*, which contains five stories the most recent of which first appeared in 1955 but is identified as "actually one of the first stories I ever wrote in my life"; the next most recent dates from 1953. Authors who have even one newer work to offer usually see to it that it finds its way into their most recent collection, and in fact most editors of such collections insist upon it.

As for novels, Sturgeon has published four since *More Than Human* (not counting a "novelization" of a movie by somebody else, from which it is only fair to look the other way); and of these only two are science fiction. The first of the four, *I, Libertine* by "Frederick R. Ewing" (Ballantine, 1956), was ostensibly written in collaboration with disc jockey-comedian Jean Shepherd, though his contribution is invisible to me. Surprisingly, the novel despite its publicity did not turn out to be a burlesque of a hairdryer or D-cup historical, but an authentic historical romance rather like those of Georgette Heyer, complexly plotted and researched up to the eyebrows. Set in 18th Century England, it's ebulliently written, witty, and has for characters a fine gallery of ripe eccentrics in the best British tradition; my favorite is Lawyer Barrowbridge, the hero's mentor.

Despite some alchemical chitchat and one chapter in which a pharmaceutical miracle is blithely committed, it contains no traces of science fiction. Considering the circumstances under which it was conceived—a deliberate attempt to create a succès de scandale by radio publicity alone—the novel is much better than anyone could have dared to hope, but it is far from being a major work.

It was followed by *Venus Plus X* (1957), a boldly experimental science-fiction novel on Sturgeon's major theme which, sadly, failed to come off. Its text is interlarded by short sketches of contemporary life, mostly upper-middle class suburban, all intended to show how the roles of the sexes are mingling and blurring even now—and good enough to show, as did "Hurricane Trio," how expertly Sturgeon could write mainstream fiction given just one editor in that field with the wit to recognize the fact. The main story deals with a trip to a never-never land, ostensibly in the future, which is a utopia populated by a race of harmonious hermaphrodites. These, it turns out, have been surgically created, involving the author in the first of a series of scientific bloopers (his major proposal is immunologically impossible*); by the end of the novel, Sturgeon, usually a model of accuracy and responsibility toward technology, has two of his major characters *watching* fall-out come down, like a display of fireworks.

But such carelessness is only a minor sample of the dangers of becoming totally bound up in a Thesis. The worst outcome, visible here, is that there is no novel when you are through. As Theodore Cogswell once remarked to me, *Venus Plus X* bears a startling resemblance to one of those common and endless Victorian utopias in which most of the action consists of taking the marvelling visitor to inspect the great Long Island and New Jersey Bridge, the gas works, the bal-

---

* I am not going to specify further because the proposal is supposed to come as a surprise. I will add, however, that the subsequent apparent success of at least one human heart transplant operation in the real world shows Sturgeon's idea to be *not* immunologically impossible—just very damned unlikely, or in other words, entirely allowable in science fiction.

loon factory, the giant telegraph center, etc., etc. Furthermore, the author of a utopia always runs the risk of finding —or worse, failing even to suspect—that the parts of his dream-world he loves best will prove repellent to his readers. Revulsion certainly overcame *me* during the chapter of this novel describing a crèche, where the descriptions of dancing children and saccharine statues reminded me of nothing so much as the artsy-craftsy nostalgicks the Southern Agrarians were peddling thirty-five years ago. (The artistic taste of the future somehow always seems as depressing as its politics, which considering our own is a pretty chilling prospect.)

The next novel was *Some of Your Blood* (1961), a fictionalized case history of an authentic vampire, on which I can report no more than that I was unable to get beyond about the first twenty pages of introductions, diary extracts, psychiatrists' reports and other apparatus.

The other science-fiction novel is a multiple-viewpoint work, technically rather like an exploded diagram of *More Than Human*, published (1958) by Dell under the abominable retitling of *The Cosmic Rape* (Sturgeon's own title, which appeared over the magazine version, was "To Marry Medusa"). It expands his vision of shared consciousness, desire and sensation between a few individuals, this time to include— though only briefly—the entire human race. This is much like the vision which climaxed Clarke's *Childhood's End*, but Clarke had the auctorial caution to bring about the actual race-wide apotheosis off-stage, as essentially incomprehensible, like an author writing of a presumably great poet who has the good sense not to "quote" any of his poems. Yet so great is Sturgeon's gift for embracing—there is no better word—all kinds of people that he almost brings off the impossible, and perhaps would have, had he hewed to the line. Instead, his novel winds up with a brief travelogue of the universe, colorful in itself but conventional, and in this context something of an anticlimax. The work is in addition quite short, probably no more than 45,000 words.

I also ought to note here a rather unaccountably neglected novella about the problems of telempathy, "The Other Man" (1956), which carries on Sturgeon's subsidiary thesis that mind-to-mind contact will increase humanity's problems, not solve them. (Sturgeon is almost the only modern science-fiction author to take this tack, though it is solidly within the tradition of the Wellsian cautionary tale.) In *More Than Human*, the multiple-person New Man was completed only by a component whose contribution was responsibility, and in a fine short story, "When You're Smiling" (1955), Sturgeon explored the hell of a man whose gift it is to feel other people's pain. The apparent villain of "The Other Man" can sense directly when other people are in trouble, and in complete opposition to the rest of his nature—which longs to be indifferent to anyone but himself—is constantly driven to their rescue. It is in effect a minor portrait of that demon of whom Goethe said he eternally willed evil, and eternally worked good. As such, it is exceedingly well done—perhaps nobody else in our field could have done it at all—but it is told from the outside, with the clue to the central character's apparent villainy saved as a surprise. The same construction was used in "When You're Smiling," and to good effect, but it cannot carry a longer story; and besides, in "When You're Smiling" we are given access to the telempath's feelings from the start, a more difficult trick to pull off but much more rewarding if it works, as in fact it does. [See also *The Issue at Hand*, p. 91.]

Sturgeon's output of new material for the magazines from 1951 through 1965—quantitatively a fair index of activity in a field where the magazines still serve as trial grounds for novels, and as a means of keeping one's name before the public—was greatest in the period 1951–1958 and then fell spectacularly, throwing his admirers into long and futile sessions of asking each other what the hell could be the matter. In the mid-Sixties he wrote two scripts for the television series *Star Trek*, but of the more than three dozen such scripts I have had the opportunity to study (as the show's adaptor, for Bantam Books), I thought them among the poorest—Sturgeon, like most masters, responds poorly to these make-work assignments, which involve the unrewarding task of being forbidden to re-think characters invented by other and lesser writers. His story in Harlan Ellison's 1967 Doubleday anthology *Dangerous Visions* (called "If All Men Were Brothers, Would You Let One Marry Your Sister?") was the first original Sturgeon in five years, an alarming gap for a man who used to exude striking and seminal stories with an apparent (if only apparent) effortlessness which was the envy of the prolific hacks in whose own dull output his work had to appear embedded.

Nevertheless, this long hiatus, or slump, or fallow period, may well be only one of those necessary explorations of blind alleys which seem to be part of the evolution of many major writers. There is still plenty of room for hope, and of the largest possible kind. The most recent previous piece of major Sturgeon to appear was the beginning of another novel, which was published in the September 1962 *F&SF* as "When You Care, When You Love," and it is totally remarkable, in theme, in characterization, in ingenuity, and in language. A quick description of its apparent subject—a young man doomed by a rare and peculiar form of cancer, who by virtue of that very disease becomes his own parents (both of them) and seems about both to relive his past in detail, and reclaim his future—no more than hints at the richness of the material, and of course cannot offer any idea of what the rest of the novel may prove to be like.

It is a fact that since the inception of modern science fiction in 1926, no single author has produced more than one masterpiece, though several have carried off more than one Hugo. From the existing text of "When You Care, When You

Love," and some discussions of it with its author, I think it more than possible that Sturgeon may be the first man to make it.

But while we are waiting, it would be well to remember that no writer, not Dostoievski, not even Shakespeare, ever managed to be all things to all men; and Theodore Sturgeon has never bothered to try. He has concentrated a lifetime into being caviar for Theodore Sturgeon, and giving the rest of us the privilege of sharing the feast. In the process, he has made himself the finest conscious artist science fiction has yet had, which is purely and simply a bonus that we had no right to expect or even to ask. We are all more in his debt than we realize, no matter what future he may bring us.

Afterword: 1969

As of late 1969, Sturgeon is reported back in production again, with five new stories. He has also published apologies for two spectacularly trashy hard-core pornographic novels by Philip José Farmer, and is rumored to be working on one himself. From his hands, such a work might even contain a few discoverable shreds of artistic merit.

VII. EXIT EUPHUES:

The Monstrosities of Merritt [1957]

WRITERS WHO UNDERTAKE STRAIGHT FANTA-sies — defined as stories with a super-natural element which is never explained away, but without, usually, any primary intent to horrify — have a marked tendency to tell them through their noses. This habit of intoning is usually attributed to an attempt to create a "poetic" atmosphere, but I think it is equally due to history — that is, the desire to make the end-product sound like Malory, Beckford, or an ancient manuscript. Sometimes, as in the case of E. R. Eddison, the result is successful, the style matching the tale and seldom getting in its way; but more often, as in H. P. Lovecraft, Clark Ashton Smith and A. Merritt, it is disastrous.

Nevertheless, Merritt apparently is still enormously popular. When Avon Books reprinted most of his work for the third time in 1957, they had sold more than a million of each of his books in their two previous reprintings. Only his estate, or the assiduous efforts of a Moskowitz, could begin to estimate what the total sales of all editions might come to.* His first real success, *The Moon Pool*, is very close to being famous; and it is indicative that when Hollywood decided to film Fritz Leiber's 1943 chiller about modern witchcraft, *Conjure Wife*, they chose to give it instead the title of a Merritt book, *Burn, Witch, Burn*. And when the critical remarks about Merritt which follow first appeared, in capsule form, in a fan magazine, the howls of *lèse majesté* were pitiful to hear.

There is evidence that the intoned style of the fantasies was a mannerism with Merritt, as opposed, for example, to that of H. P. Lovecraft, who told everything in about the same tone of voice. When Merritt wanted to write a story in which the fantasy elements were of relatively minor importance, or were to be explained away, his prose lost many of its kinks. This is apparent, for instance, in *Seven Footprints to Satan*. This is the style which Moskowitz called "restrained, almost journalistic in tone." Brian Aldiss has teased Moskowitz for the characteristic infelicity of this formulation, but there is a certain amount of justice hidden in it; compared to the style of the fantasies, that of *Satan* shows much less effort to be "poetic," and is more closely reportorial, which probably is what Moskowitz meant. It is certainly an improvement upon that of Merritt's contemporary Sax Rohmer, upon whose Dr. Fu-Manchu *Satan* was apparently modelled.

---

* For some reason, despite the popularity of the books, Avon in 1957 seemed embarrassed by their antiquity—to the point of hiding their dates of first publication in Roman numerals. By 1963, when Avon had been taken over by Hearst, however, the dates came out into the clear.

Merritt seldom showed this much restraint, however. *The Moon Pool* (1919) is almost unreadable now—stuffy, empty and dated; and its sequel, *Conquest of the Moon Pool*, is no better. Their magic, whatever it may have been forty-five years ago, has vanished with time. The style is both windy and cliché-ridden, as well as being ungrammatical with great frequency. The scientific rationale—again, regardless of how convincing it may have seemed in 1919, when terms like magnetism and radioactivity were apparently being allowed to mean anything an author found it convenient, like Humpty Dumpty, to say that they meant—has been turned by time into nonsense. The characters are stock: a fey Irish-American, a pedantic professor, a Scandinavian sailor who invokes Norse gods, the perennial Russian spy, and so on. (In successive rewrites, of which Merritt did many, his Russian villains often got changed into Germans, and then back into Russians again in a determined attempt to keep the clichés current.)

The major trouble with *The Moon Pool*, however, lies elsewhere; other fantasies have survived faults as serious, in the sense that it is still possible to read them without one's eyes glazing over by page 68. The difference is that Merritt's novel is not about anything; it has no central idea to draw its events together. Unlike the similarly wooden fantasies of Haggard, or the similarly overwritten fantasies of C. A. Smith, *The Moon Pool* appears to be purely a private work, written out of Merritt's dream life and using images which may have had pith and system for him—though even that concession is difficult to defend in the face of the deadness of the novel— but which the reader cannot share. Indeed, the only attempt Merritt made to give the reader access to them was to cram them into a completely predictable plot with cardboard inhabitants.

Why, then, has this crude performance been so highly touted for so many years? Nostalgia may provide one answer; and the book does contain a certain amount of misty sensuality, some derring-do, and a number of faraway places with strange-sounding names. It is also the perfect demonstration that these three standard ingredients of romantic fantasy cannot produce a good book all by themselves.

The Metal Monster (1920) was the immediate successor to the two Moon Pool novels, whose protagonist is also the protagonist of this one. This novel was probably the most frequently and extensively revised of all Merritt's works, though none of the revisions ever made it popular, and hence the final version available shows Merritt having made some gains as a craftsman, particularly in characterization. His witch-women, of course, are all alike, no matter in what novel you find them; but at least, he had given up his earlier typing of his merely human characters with regional funny hats, and they begin to talk like vaguely human beings, too.

The idea of the Metal Monster itself — a hive creature whose individuals are assorted mobile geometrical solids, which can fit themselves together into any desired functional shape—is far above the intellectual level of the Moon Pool novels, and Merritt does some striking things with it (most of them expectable to a modern reader, but this by itself is not a fair complaint). Up to this point, however, Merritt's plotting was still crude and rambling, and the revisions never met this difficulty head-on. The journey which gets the characters onto the scene of the action takes 72 of the Avon edition's 222 pages, most of them dull, and the action itself is wholly arbitrary.

By the publication of *The Ship of Ishtar* (1924), it has become clear that Merritt has arrived at a list of standard ingredients for his fantasies. This consists of a beginning in the present, a far journey or dream gimmick, a never-never land, a quasi-numinous Thing, an evil priest, a beautiful temptress, occult powers deriving from the Thing, much swordplay (guns invariably turn out to be useless), and layer upon layer of overloaded purple prose. Having settled all this, Merritt apparently went to sleep for the next 220 pages, for *The Ship of Ishtar* is the weakest of them all.

To begin with, the imaginative pressure is low; the novel is devoid of the kind of central poetic idea which could occasionally evoke from Merritt his poor best, so that the plot quickly becomes little more than a succession of palace intrigues, as difficult to follow and as inherently uninteresting as a scramble of yarn produced by a kitten. Secondly, the setting is derived—for lack of a Thing—from ancient history, a subject about which Merritt had standard romantic notions unencumbered by any factual knowledge whatever. This makes the *Ship* even more preposterous than usual.

Perhaps Merritt himself sensed this. Whatever the reason, by 1928 he had produced *Seven Footprints to Satan*, which as noted above is unlike his usual fantasies in many respects. In addition to being better written, it has a tight plot whose surprises emerge logically from previously-planted material— also unlike Sax Rohmer's books, which were slapped hastily together from independent magazine stories, and show it. The characters are still stock, but they come out of a different trunk than Merritt usually favored, though family resemblances are evident. Satan himself is a delightful villain, more ingenious than Fu-Manchu, better motivated, and above all more complex; Merritt even takes some pains to make the reader like him at several points, a sure sign of a writer with his full attention on his work. There is no magic; the plot is impelled forward primarily by human greed, abetted by drug addiction and the device of the Seven Footprints, which turn out to be—no, I will stop here, because there is still a chance that some readers of mine haven't encountered this book yet, and it is in my judgment the one Merritt novel which still remains worth reading. It also turned out to be immensely popular; the Avon edition alone went through nine printings between 1942 and 1963. Stylistically, *Burn, Witch, Burn* belongs to the same canon.

The pull of romantic fantasy, however, proved irresistible. I shall consider only one more of those here: *The Face in the Abyss* (1931). It is the mixture as before. The technique has improved slightly: the novel gets down to business a little faster (after 52 of 253 pages) than does *The Metal Monster*, after introducing three wholly unnecessary characters who have to be eliminated a few pages later. All the usual props and types are trotted out. The scientific underpinning, just barely fair even in its day, has been rendered ridiculous by the intervening years. The language in which it is told is lavishly colorful but so imprecise that the reader often finds it impossible to visualize what Merritt thinks he is describing, and the author's fondness for rare or obsolete words like "cadent" and "squattering," though not quite as obtrusive as C. A. Smith's, makes his purple passages even more mannered and stagy.

The central idea was a good one. Nobody who has read the book is ever likely to forget the first confrontation with the Face of the title, a vast, satanic stone mask which constantly sweats, drools and weeps molten gold. But Merritt promptly proceeds to destroy this brooding, frightening symbol by making a man-sized parody of it the villain of the novel. The plot then disintegrates into the usual welter of swordplay and palace intrigue. To have realized that vision of evil would have taken a poet, and Merritt was only rarely —say, once per book—a poet. What his fans call his poetry turns out to be thousands of yards of flowery, unselective prose. To do him justice, here is a sample,* which was quoted at me by the admirer who most bitterly resented my criticism of the man:

> "What do you want with me, Yolara?" Larry asked hoarsely.
> "Nay," came the mocking voice. "Not Yolara to you, Larree —call me by those sweet names you taught me—Honey of the Wild Bee-s-s, Net of Hearts—" Again her laughter tinkled.... The

* From *The Conquest of the Moon Pool*, I believe.

fiendishness died from the eyes; they grew blue, wondrous; the veil of invisibility slipped down from the neck, the shoulders, half revealing the gleaming breasts. And weird, weird beyond all telling was that exquisite head and bust floating there in air—and beautiful, sinisterly beautiful beyond all telling, too. So even might Lilith, the serpent woman, have shown herself tempting Adam!

The prosecution rests.

And yet, and yet—there are still all those sales. I cannot help but be appalled at the discovery (not new with me, I am sure, but still unsettling) that a novelist with this large an audience, and among fans a reputation to match, should have so many major and minor flaws. At the time I first sat down to draft these remarks, I had in line of duty read (or reread) four Merritt novels in as many months, and it was possible that the jaundice inspired in me by all these stage Irishmen, tinkling revenants and wooden images was simply the result of an overdose. But I don't think that this explains very much. Good fiction never produces that sensation of having eaten too much cotton candy, no matter how many times one rereads it.

The inescapable fact is that the books were trash to begin with, though they might have been better. Of the novels discussed here,* both *The Metal Monster* and *The Face in the Abyss* have possible central subjects, of which the objects named in the titles are potent and striking symbols. Yet Merritt apparently never suspected this, threw away his opportunity at once, and instead wrote just another empty romance enswathed in Deep Purple.

The emperor's new clothes are there, more or less; but there is no emperor inside.

---

* Merritt wrote only ten novels—plus seven short stories—and of these seven are mentioned above; the remaining ones are *Creep, Shadow, Creep*, *Dwellers in the Mirage*, and *The Snake Mother*.

VIII. SCATTERSHOT:
Practice Makes Perfect—
But It Can Also Cut Your Throat [1957]

FROM THE PROFESSIONAL WRITER'S POINT OF view, the primary interest in *Astounding Science Fiction* [now, as *Analog*, as then] continues to center on the editor's preoccupation with extra-sensory powers and perceptions ("psi") as a springboard for stories. By my rough count, 113 pages of the total editorial content of the January and February 1957 issues of this magazine are devoted to psi, and 172 pages to non-psi material. This would be dull enough for readers not sharing Mr. Campbell's enthusiasm, but even these figures probably do him a favor he doesn't have coming. I arrived at them by crediting the first installment of a serial of my own, "Get Out of My

Sky," to the non-psi side of the ledger, but this is not quite fair, since as an entity the yarn—the second installment of which is psionic in focus—would certainly be judged a psi story. With this allowed for, the total for these first two issues of 1957 is 145 pages of psi text, and 140 pages of non-psi.

The Eric Frank Russell novelette "Nuisance Value" is non-psi. It is the third of three long *ASF* stories of the period to propose that apparently helpless military prisoners can bollix up their powerful captors crucially; one of the earlier yarns was also by Russell, the other by Christopher Anvil. The theme appears to be made to order for Russell's gleeful iconoclasm, and true enough, the first story was funny. The Anvil piece was only mildly so, and this third go-around on the idea just leaves it gasping, exhausted and bleeding from the mushy little ball of wishful thinking which lay at its core all along. "Nuisance Value" in particular gives its protagonists a push-over for a problem, by making the very idea of an escape-attempt inconceivable to their jailors. (This story later appeared as half of an Ace double novel, under the title *The Space Willies*. Separated in time from its siblings, it seems a good deal funnier, though the central flaw of course remains.)

H. Beam Piper's "Omnilingual" is also non-psi. The central problem here is that of translating a long-dead Martian language, and Piper attacks it in sophisticated fashion. His point is that translating a tongue which belonged to a scientific culture is a problem inherently different from, and in the long run easier than, translating a pre-scientific language—because the basic clues are not philological, but physical. This is probably true, though Piper makes some assumptions about continuity of symbols which I think doubtful.

A more fundamental objection, however, is that this long story has almost no content *as a story*, despite its technological interest. The gimmick about the problem of translation is the center of the piece, rather than being, as it should, an important part of the background. The human relationships are thinly sketched, trite, remote from basic human emotions, and never at any point as interesting as the technicalities are. There is plenty of intellection in "Omnilingual," but virtually no insight.

I raise this point because I think there is no inherent reason why a story *has* to be dull because of its intellectual frame— even a psi story. But when an editor becomes convinced that a concept like psi is more than just a device—that it is *real*— then he becomes more interested in the gimmick-thinking than he is in the fiction. This is an old problem in science fiction, but it becomes acute when the editor's intent is frankly pedagogical.

The Blish serial, "Get Out of My Sky," which later led off a 1960 Crest paperback of the same title, sets up a political situation drifting toward nuclear war on an imaginary planet called Home, which has become even more unbalanced by the discovery of a sister-planet, Rathe, which also harbors intelligent life. Both planets are largely deserts (of water on Home, of sand on Rathe) and have nothing to gain by fighting each other, but Aidregh, Home's chief politician, is having a hard time resisting his local warhawks. In a desperate gesture, he accepts an invitation from the Rathe leader to "go to Korea," where with the aid of psionic training he becomes a more effective politician and returns to Home to resume his campaign against the impending war with more hope.

This is a slender argument to carry a 30,000-word story, and in order to keep things going Blish has concentrated chiefly on the emotional conflicts within Aidregh, as they are variously triggered by his opposition, his son and the son's girl, the girl's father—a physician who plays the role of a Greek chorus to the story—and Rathe's head-of-state, Margent; and, of course, by the pressure of his responsibilities to the peoples of both planets. These are mostly expectable, however, so that the main burden of the story *still* devolves upon its background, that is, upon those parts of the situation which derive from its fantasy content and not from its analogies with present-day Earthly international politics.

The result—and it is rather an odd one—is that the most interesting half of the story is the second, which is where the the psi content is concentrated, because it is here that the background material is most novel. Blish has borrowed to good effect a trick of Lester del Rey, who never describes a faster-than-light space drive—or a similar standard prop—without working out, for each new story, a new rationale for it, thus making the gimmick his own rather than (as is usually the case with lesser writers) a magical device for *avoiding* thought. In this instance, Blish's explanation of how psi powers might work differs completely from that proposed in his only other major flight on the subject (*Jack of Eagles*, Greenberg, 1952)—but what is more important, it also differs completely from any proposed by his editor (Campbell) up to that time.

Hence, although Blish's intent here was precisely to do what Piper failed to do, the residual effect of "Get Out of My Sky" closely resembles that of "Omnilingual": both are stronger on ingenuity than on strictly fictional values. If there is a moral, it is that there is more than one way to make the same mistake.

As for the psi-based short stories in these two issues, they suffer uniformly from a failure to take any real interest in the characters, with the exception of "Unlucky Chance" by M. C. Pease. Here a dull-minded woman meets two aliens, discovers that she has psi powers, and scares both them and herself into fits. Summarized that baldly, the plot sounds like any of the twenty-odd exercises in cuteness around a similar theme— mostly involving little old ladies on rural front porches—that *F&SF* and Bradbury's imitators used to specialize in, but it is worth noting that Pease *did* try to set up his story primarily as a human problem, centered upon his reluctant and dim-

brained central character; whether or not it comes off for you
depends on whether or not you find his protagonist too dull
to be interesting in herself. It's supernally difficult to make
an intentionally dull woman interesting in spite of herself,
and I think Pease lacked the skill to bring it off, but it was
an honest attempt.

Stanley Mullen's "The Man With the Corkscrew Mind," on
the other hand, shows that he has learned nothing important
about the craft of fiction since his over-blown, idiot-plotted
1951 novel. The plot—a man set to trap a telepathic alien
turns out to be a telepath himself, to his own surprise—is
ancient, and not improved in the retelling. The dialogue is
devoted mostly to crisscross lecturing for the benefit of the
reader, so pompous in tone as to suggest that what you are
reading is really a Perelman burlesque. The setting in a mental
hospital is ill-imagined, and full of Mullen's familiar idiocies
(violent patients are quartered on the ward floor; isolation
cells turn out to be unlocked at exactly the wrong moment;
attendants are brutal and stupid in the presence of the doctor
in charge, and go unreproved for it; the alien could bolt the
hospital at any time, but waits until a moment of maximum
danger for him.) The expository sections are over-written,
loaded with imprecise words and with such clumsy devices as
dropping into the second person. The appearance of a story
this ill-carpentered in a major magazine like *ASF* is an implied rebuke to every writer in the field who is struggling to
perfect his craftsmanship; nor can there be any possible claim
that its thematic interest—it has none—compensates for its
ineptness.

Poul Anderson's "Security Risk" is at least readable; Anderson is never less than skillful. It has a mechanically competent plot, with a small snapper at the end. However, it
does nothing with its psi frame but graft the old alternate-
Earths hypothesis onto it, and does not provide any rationale
for either. As idea-fiction it is thus an exercise in the inter-

weaving of clichés; and its emotional content is limited to an echo of F. B. Long's old girl-in-the-moon dream-tales. Any man with Anderson's colossal productivity (his section of the *MIT Index 1951-65* has 156 entries!) has to be forgiven an occasional misfire; this is surely one of them.

C. L. Cottrell's "For the First Time" gives us an immortal man turned into a moron by lobotomy, who got his immortality from a faith-healer in one of five possible ways—no one of which is more than mentioned, let alone defended. Its emotional content is kept at the lowest possible level by presenting this potentially pitiable human being as nothing more than a problem in life-insurance payments.

Lee Correy, in "The Education of Icky," reduces the whole question of psi to that of a djinn who talks jive-talk with singular inaccuracy and no excuse, and has to be sent to a university before he can hope to understand modern science even as well as Correy does. The idea is wholly irresponsible to begin with, and it is executed with nauseating archness.

That leaves us with nothing but "The War Is Over" by Algis Budrys, usually a dependable performer even at his most minor; and his is the only short story in these two issues which is non-psi. However: it is a puzzle-piece, the solution to which comes out of the author's hat. When it finally emerges, it turns out to be a golem. Since this is not (to put the matter gently) a new idea, since Budrys has only a minute variation on it to offer us, since the variation itself comes unequipped with any rationale, and since the plot is so set up as to lead the reader to expect that it will be emptied of emotion by the ending (as indeed it is) . . . all these things being so, we will have to agree sadly that the whole thing is no more than a thin notion thinly executed — a sort of aborted sneeze.

Budrys at his worst is a serious technician with an unfailing ear for the language. This makes him look like a master next to Correy and Mullen, men who have no real knowledge of

English, let alone fiction. But is this enough? A magazine like *ASF*, I submit, ought to be demanding the best of a writer like Budrys—not just making his weakest work look good by publishing it embedded in trash.

Unfortunately, these days Mr. Campbell seems to be more interested in education than in fiction—not a new situation for him, but no less deplorable for being familiar. What he has failed to see is that this position is untenable even heuristically; he is using the wrong tools for the job even on his own terms.

Fiction should enlarge our understanding of our fellows first of all, or it will be entirely replaced by non-fiction, which can easily embrace every other function that communication serves. Now, it seems to me, Mr. Campbell is in a position to ignore this primary function of fiction more completely than ever before, because he believes that it is possible to short-circuit the process, and create rapport with "psi powers" and "psi machines." I think he is wrong, but that is not the central issue anyhow. What is important is that such powers and machines are the antithesis of fiction. Fiction writers who help Mr. Campbell to propagate them and the myth they serve are cutting their own throats.

To be sure, psi can be a good subject for stories; there are no bad subjects. But I submit that we dare not let ourselves be cajoled into becoming Assistant Propagandists instead of fiction-writers, as Campbell's powerful personality is constantly persuading us to do. If there is to be any hope for us, we ought to remain stubbornly more interested in our own opinions than in his.

At this point—partly in memoriam, but partly also because it offers me an opportunity to expand my sermon above—let's look at two now-extinct Columbia magazines, *Science Fiction Stories* for May 1957, and *Future* for Spring 1957. Only one of the fifteen stories in these two issues is even worth recalling now on its merits [speaking as of 1968], though all but one of them are by writers now well known either as themselves or under pennames—some were old pros even then; and the only other story of the fifteen that comes close to being dragged back across the years was by the only newcomer in the group. I shall speak highly here of the good story and the nearly good one; but some of the demerits are worth recalling, too, since they are still quite applicable to current practice.

If only to stay in character, let me start with a demerit, and for an instantly defensible reason: the poor thing is psionic, and the passage of ten years has still not rid us of a vast over-production of non-writing about this non-subject. The 1957 story in recall is "Extra Space Perception," by Russ (or as he used to sign himself, R. R.) Winterbotham. Though the story as fiction was a disaster, it might have been notable as the first piece of science fiction to reach print which tried to take advantage of a real and serious attempt to explain telepathy from a rational model within the accepted frames of physics, even including the inverse-square and conservation-of-energy laws. This was called the telepathic quantum hypothesis, which in Winterbotham's story is called "Teq."

The Teq hypothesis (to adopt Winterbotham's shorthand) suggested that *if* a center for the detection of telepathy existed within the brain, it might be activated by the reception of a single quantum of energy (presumably of a highly penetrating kind), acting as an organic detector like an electroscope or a Geiger counter which is sensitive to even tiny touches of ionizing radiation, like the eardrum which is sometimes held to respond to the impact of even a single molecule of air, or like the eye which is reached by single photons and reacts to them (within its frequency range) with enormous sensitivity. The model was an honest attempt to satisfy the often-raised objection to telepathy that its described behavior violated the inverse-square law.

The model failed. As anyone who has been through high-school physics can see, it was loaded with *ad hoc* assumptions, and moreover it contained many appeals to analogy which did not hold up. (For example, while it is true that a single quantum of light does reach the retina with nearly undiminished energy, this does not answer the objection from the inverse-square law, because one photon is far below the energy level necessary to activate the visual purple; a man receiving just one photon is as blind as a man receiving none. The appeal to hearing was even less tenable, for even should it be true that the eardrum can detect the impact of one molecule—which is in itself a purely speculative proposition —the energetics involved in such an impact are of a wholly different order of magnitude and obey wholly different laws, one set belonging to quantum mechanics, the other to classical mechanics, between which there is no crossover at all.)

Now, I do *not* require any (let alone every) science-fiction writer to be a theoretical physicist. But if he is going to invoke a scholium like this to support a story, I think he ought to have some minimum knowledge of the rules of the game —just as I would ask a man who sets out to write a story based in chess not to treat the game as if it were a form of tick-tack-toe. Furthermore, it ought to be exciting for a science-fiction writer to be the first man to have in his hands a model for telepathy which really looked like it might be made to work, and out of which he might therefore wring a story which was also unique, not only in its metaphysical assumptions, but in its dramatic consequences.

But all Winterbotham gave us was the usual tick-tack-toe. The fact that the model does not work should have been only a minor drawback—after all, none of them do, and if science-fiction models worked we should be up to our necks in anti-gravity and tractor beams by now; it could have been made to *sound* as if it worked. Instead, Winterbotham uses it only as a vocabulary for a few magic words, so as a rationale for his story it quickly disintegrates into transparent foolishness. Worse, his characters never seem to feel any identifiable emotions, and they are involved in a plot which resembles closely the most idiotic Western you ever read.

This story, and quite a few of the others in these two issues, well represent one of the standard penalties of having the lowest rate of pay in the field, even for an editor of Lowndes' dedication, taste and skill: all too often, you get to be a pasture for spavined horses.

In the same issue, a short story by Irving E. Cox, Jr., "The Janus City," must be equally thoroughly and deservedly forgotten now, but it had in fact one modest claim to interest: It was an almost perfect example of one kind of "fan fiction"—a term often used in denigration but seldom defined. In my experience about 85 percent of fan fiction is characterized by a confusion between stupidity and tragedy. (The other 15 percent is too incompetent to make it possible to say what it's characterized by.) A stupid man who blacks his own eye on an obvious doorknob is not a tragic figure, but a clown—yet most young writers (Cox had first appeared slightly more than five years earlier) seem to feel that there is something heavily, wisely ironic in their pictures of the stumblings of knaves. The essence of the matter is this: *Only a whole man can be a tragic figure.*

This lesson is emphasized, as a matter of fact, by a story in the Spring 1957 *Future* by Richard Wilson, called "The In-Betweens." Wilson, a newspaperman for many years, has both by training and by temperament been incapable of writing any less than professionally since about 1940, but we all fall into traps now and then. The plot of this story is reminiscent of that of Nat Schachner's "The Isotope Men" (*Astounding Stories*, January 1936). Wilson's version is shorter, more sophisticated, makes at least some scientific sense and is better written. Nevertheless, the primary notion—fragmenting a human being into separate physical entities each one of which represents a single human trait—is a pseudo-problem to begin with, since the real problem of human nature is its complexity, and the only honest solution to the fragmented-man story would be to show that it makes a bad situation worse. Wilson does not do this, but instead supplies an ending which is inconsistent even with his own premises: one of his fragments turns out to be a genuinely complex character!

This issue also contains two successes. One is Carol Emsh-willer's "The Hunting Machine," which is a prime example of what Lowndes' receptivity could do for the field when it was hitting on all eight.* I deplore [today as well as back then] most of the lady authors in science fiction, and the lady men who are imitating them, but Mrs. Emshwiller is not a lady author. She is an author, period. "The Hunting Machine" is very brief, but it shook me down to my shoes. It is a lineal descendant of the man-against-nature stories of such writers as Jack London and Ernest Thompson Seton, in which the author is on nature's side. It is, however, a thoroughly mod-ern version; its subject is alienation—the increasing shallow-ness, callousness and coarseness by which man pays for an increasingly complex machine civilization. This is a big sub-ject, which she has packed into a small space—about the size of a sledgehammer head.

The other success is "The Mile," by John Tara, which describes, with considerable effect, the thoughts of a baby being born only to die immediately thereafter (though he never says that is what he is doing; the editor tells you, prob-ably perforce for this audience). This has been done before (most notably by Maude Hutchins) in the mainstream, and this version contains nothing which would convert the idea

---

* Lowndes was the first editor to print this author ("This Thing Called Love," in a 1955 *Future*). This is just the kind of exercise of editorial originality which kept him in business for years despite his publisher's penny-pinching; see also *The Issue at Hand*, pp. 47-8. It is ridiculous that this man should now be left editing only a string of even less promising magazines which subsist upon 30-year-old reprints!

into a science-fiction story, but the point of view attributed to the baby——a sort of stew of mangled scraps of knowledge, philosophy and Village cynicism——is startling, despite the author's fondness for bootless tricks with clichés. If this author is a beginner——as the text suggests that he may be—— he can go nowhere from this beginning but out of science fiction, and the sooner the better; he is too good even raw to be bothered with a protracted adolescence at wonder-mongering.* I hope this is exactly the case, for a writer who is capable of suggesting that apparently healthy babies may die at birth because they have *already* had enough of the human condition is a man who should spend a minimum of time talking about cryotrons, thermionic valves and imaginary problems; people who can talk meaningfully about the human condition are in frighteningly short supply.

Endnote: Lowndes tells me that "Tara" was the well-known science-fiction fan and sometime author (mostly as "Hugh Raymond"), John B. Michel. I think my jaw must have hung open for at least two days after this revelation.

---

* Tara has no entry in the Day *Index*, and only one—this story—in the *MIT Index*.

IX. SCIENCE-FANTASY
AND TRANSLATIONS:
Two More Cans of Worms [1960, 1963]

IN *THE ISSUE AT HAND* (P. 112) I NOTED THAT
Avram Davidson, then editor of *F&SF*,
once classified five of the stories in the
August 1962 issue of his magazine as "science-fantasy,"
which I called "a term specially revived by his predecessor,"
Robert P. Mills, "(independently of H. G. Wells, who meant
something else by it) to cover the Aldiss 'Hothouse' series."
Later in the Sixties, the term came to be widely used as a
label for the A. Merritt kind of story—not true sword-and-
sorcery text, but the kind of yarn in which nobody is supposed to care about gross scientific errors and inconsistencies

because they are covered over with great gobs of color and rhetoric.

I am not trying to legislate this kind of story out of existence or anathematize its writers, as Algis Budrys in 1963 gently suggested that I might be. But I do think it has gotten out of hand; and though I cannot and would not order the tide to turn back, I can see no virtue in our squeezing our eyes shut and calling it Muroc Dry Lake, either.

Wells used the term originally to cover what we would today call "hard" science fiction, in which a conscientious attempt to be faithful to already known facts (as of the date of writing) was the substrate on which the story was to be built, and if the story was also to contain a miracle, it ought at least not to contain a whole arsenal of them. Today it is being used as an excuse for getting the facts wrong, and it seems perfectly clear to me that a man with no respect for facts (scientific or otherwise) is going to be too poor a reporter to write acceptable fiction, at least much of the time. As Sprague de Camp pointed out in *Science-Fiction Handbook*, once a reader catches an author at being wrong about a point, no matter how small, the credibility of all the rest of the story is damaged, and he may begin to wonder if more than just the facts are being scamped.

This is precisely what happened in the Hothouse series, a sadly damaged piece of goods. Aldiss had a marvellous idea; he clothed it in highly personal, highly cadenced prose; he filled it with lovely ingenuities; and he lost control of it. He has responded to criticisms of his impossible celestial mechanics by saying that he is Brian Aldiss, not Isaac Asimov.* This is not a good defense. And the infernal mechanics are only the beginning. The late Richard McKenna has pointed

---

* In "Hothouse," the Moon is said to have stopped circling the Earth and to have taken up an orbit around the Sun by which it moves parallel to the Earth and remains stationary above a single point on the Earth, permitting among other things a rope to be let down from the Moon to the Earth. Budrys was asked by

out that the fiction, too, is riddled with contradictions and just plain lapses of memory [many of them, however, repaired in the novel version]. The stories have many virtues, beyond all question; but "a reasonably successful attempt at *systematic* imagination" [Budrys' phrase, my emphasis] they are not.

Can it reasonably be said, of the demand that a writer get checkable matters right, that [as Budrys suggested] it is a case of "inapplicable special standards"?

Yes—if outright fantasy is what we know we are talking about. The Hothouse stories can adopt this exit only in an emergency. Quite frequently they turn upon facts of biology which Aldiss *has* got right, and which would have been disastrous for his story had he gotten them wrong. The whole point of the modern usage of the term "science-fantasy," it seems to me, is to define a kind of hybrid in which plausibility is specifically invoked for most of the story, but may be cast aside in patches at the author's whim and according to no visible system or principle.

Wells went beyond the facts, but he had an operating principle to which he was almost Calvinistically faithful: he allowed himself only one miracle per work, and insisted of his own performance that it exploit even that miracle logically. The rest of the text in a given work had to be as true to the scientific knowledge of his time as he could manage. Jules Verne certainly would not have agreed with this characterization (in fact, he thought Wells' romances utterly fantastic), but then, Verne was playing it safe; he seldom wrote about anything which wasn't already on the engineers' drawing-boards, and so has a nearly undeserved reputation for predicting things which, in fact, he knew to be already in existence,

---

Mills, who bought the original stories, if this disqualified the stories as science fiction; Budrys emphatically said it did. Mills then asked Asimov if any repairs could be made in the assumption which would save the situations in the stories; Asimov said no. Ballistically, indeed, the assumption is utter nonsense.

and not always only *in posse* . . . and at the same time, he frequently fell all over his technological feet. Wells looked much
farther into the future—yet, except for a few relapses into
the outright impossible (about which he really should have
known better—like Cavorite—though people like Thomas
Alva Edison were similarly naive at the time), he kept his
text as "hard" as any purist who also demands good fiction
of a fiction-writer could demand.

In his time, this kind of rigor was welcome, because it
added credibility to what was otherwise only a faith. This
was the worship of Progress, a much more powerful religion
than any of the official ones in his lifetime; and the early
science-fiction writers were its prophets.

That is, they were its prophets so long as they were hopeful. The dark side of Wells was ignored, though he tried very
earnestly from the beginning to make it known. In particular, he said firmly that the first seven of his science-fiction
novels were derived from Swift. I for one find it hard to
understand how anyone reading *The Island of Dr. Moreau*
could miss its explicit subjugation to the horse chapter of
Gulliver's Travels, with all the black devices there in the same
order, all the horror at the animal side of man intact—
indeed, hardly even rewritten toward the end. What *is*
astonishing is that someone like Colin Wilson should think
these novels optimistic, and that Wells' last book, *Mind at
the End of Its Tether*, should impress him as a surprising
revelation of misanthropy and pessimism suddenly arrived at,
either out of nowhere in a reversal of Wells' character, or in
revulsion against a lifetime of sunny prophecy.

Wells to be sure had his turn at trying to educate mankind
and write self-fulfilling prophecies; all the Fabians did. Yet
Tether differs from *Moreau* and *The Time Machine* only in
its audience, not in its purport. In between there were also
some "straight" or "mainstream" novels, but these were
hardly more hopeful. What is probably the best known of

them, *Tono-Bungay*, puts us on notice that Wells expected the best non-scientific brains of mankind to use the name of science only for fraud. This line of thought reaches a climax in a mordant character study, *The Bulpington of Blup*, an account of a compulsive liar with fake-scientific leanings which shows the worst sides of the dreams the engineer-romanticizers fed on (between Lisbon earthquakes). In short, these too were cautionary tales upon the Swiftian model—but now being set in commonplace contemporary settings, not in Laputa or on a desert island or the far future or the Moon.

What extraordinary stuff to be writing for audiences fed on Bellamy and similar utopians! But the audience saw then only the wonderful predictions—airplanes, atomic bombs, land iron-clads, truth gas, invisibility, space travel, time travel, and all the rest of that spectrum of notions—remarkably few of them still unrealized—which confirmed in advance its worship of Progress. That audience resolutely refused to see that Wells, when he was not pushing free love or total honesty or some other such panacea (which was far less often than the usual capsule dismissal of him would lead you to believe) did not really think that any changes in gadgets, backdrops or bureaucracies were likely to change human behaviour. When he wanted to fake such a change, he dropped technology and resorted to a *really* major miracle, imposed not by Science but from Outside—and people still say, vaguely, that these science-fiction novels (*In the Days of the Comet* is the type case) were his poorest. But they failed to heed the tears shed in the best, though they were copious.

And how extraordinary, too, that he is still not given credit for them . . .*

It is seductive to attribute the rise in sloppiness in science

---

* Jack Williamson's doctorate thesis, *H. G. Wells, Critic of Progress*, does go into this question in detail, as its title indicates. The thesis was submitted in 1966, and ran in five parts in *Riverside Quarterly*, beginning in that journal's first issue of 1968 (Vol. 3, No. 1).

fiction entirely to the influence of individual writers like Merritt, or freak best-sellers like *The Moon Pool*, but we need to be reminded that there had to be some reason for the popularity of such works, and it cannot be found in accuracy, characterization, construction, mastery of language or any of the other canons we so often invoke. Furthermore, even much later, American science fiction in its finest period, which most critics—including this one—center around the 1940's, was almost entirely hopeful, much more like Verne than like Wells. (John W. Campbell even today tends to resist a story which shows aliens defeating human beings, or otherwise suggests that a given situation may indeed be hopeless or a problem insoluble, though he does nevertheless print such stories if he finds them compelling on other grounds; and very late in 1967, Frederik Pohl also demanded that his writers begin to come up with solutions instead of problems.)

During that same period, American science fiction was almost entirely "hard"; the best writers of that decade tried to be as respectful of the facts as Wells had been (sometimes to the extinction of the story proper, but this is not a criticism of the philosophy but only of its practitioners).

Very well. Why has that attitude now changed so markedly that most of the best science-fiction writers of the 1960's are markedly down in the mouth, and at the same time do not really think it important if they bollix up the facts in the service of their vision?

The first question is the easiest to answer. The times were not as hopeful as we in the United States still thought they were; and of course the number of science-fiction writers who had read the major prophetic novelists of our own era, men like Céline and Kafka, was tiny and still is (sneering at people who take Kafka seriously is a favorite gambit of an appalling majority of science-fiction *writers*, as well as readers —all the more appalling because it is quite clear from what they say that they are judging from jacket blurbs or even more third-hand material). After a while, however, even the most sophisticated writers of hopeful science fiction also found themselves selling sophisticated horror stories, written with obvious relish for their favorite editor, who had also adopted magic and still cherishes it today (though he continues to call it science).

Wells wrote stories about magic too, and also with relish; but always by his hard rule—hardest, of course, upon himself, but he was not a lazy author—that only a single fantastic assumption was admissible per story, and must thereafter be developed with the strictest logic of which the writer is capable. Most writers of fantasy, on the other hand, adopt the idiom in a blind and grateful *abandonment* of the life of the mind. Most science-fiction writers today are prosecuting the same sort of one-handed adultery, under the impression that they are uttering a public protest or a social criticism, to cheers from Kingsley Amis and others.

These science-fiction writers have adopted Wells' despairing view of the uses humanity would probably make of science (and I certainly cannot declare that they are wrong in so doing); but they have utterly rejected Wells' respect for the facts themselves, and so are systematically falsifying any claim they might have had upon the respect and attention of the reader.

These writers decided in advance that rockets were only going to multiply tragedy; that the new planets we visited would defeat us if they were hostile, and that we would defile them if they weren't; that we could expect nothing from television but brain-washing, nothing from atomic energy but explosions and lung cancer, nothing from universal literacy but book-burning, nothing from better medicine but over-population, nothing from . . . But there is nothing wrong with these propositions, experience should have taught us already, but the word "nothing"; except for that, they can be defended at some length.

I want to repeat here, AT THE TOP OF MY VOICE, that I am not attempting to dictate any other writer's attitudes or choice of subject.

If these writers even wish to make the general case—*The future of Progress is universal human degradation*—that can be defended too, with a little care, and they can enlist Wells to support it. But Wells took pains to be precise, and if possible, right, about the ways in which it might happen, and the facts which already pointed in that direction. The annoying thing about the modern romantics of science fiction is not the moral they preach, but the fact that they seem to take almost equally great pains to be wrong, even about what is *already* known. They have passed from fiction to pamphleteering, from art to advertising.

I continue to feel that the Mars of Ray Bradbury, or the celestial mechanics of *Hothouse*, is as false a territory as the America of Ilya Ehrenburg, and therefore doing just as great a disservice to Bradbury's or Aldiss' real content; much the same thing could be said of the "science" of J. G. Ballard, who like Bradbury and Aldiss is also a poet and therefore must command our attention.

If science fiction is to have any value as social criticism, or as moral paradigm, or as real examination and prediction of human behavior, or any of the other special virtues it has claimed for itself, it has damn well got to be believable above almost any other possible form of expression. Otherwise, the burden of the story, *whatever* it may be, will not carry conviction, and the whole operation of writing it becomes at best only a game for children, at worst a piece of cynical buck-turning on a par with lying about the virtues of one indistinguishable brand of hair-oil over another. Wells knew this, and he practised in accordance with the knowledge, though he *shared* the moral gloom of our chiefest modern fable-smiths in the idiom he invented almost all by himself.

I have philosophical preferences here which I must be

frank about. I do not think that Progress is entirely a foredoomed faith, though I do agree that it is *only* a faith now
and defending it is an exercise of almost Scholastic complexity (and, perhaps, futility). But I have some knowledge
of some sciences; I have already seen some social good come
of atomic energy (to face the major of all the bogey-men);
greater and more astonishing good things might yet emerge
from other technologies, and other, as yet almost completely
abstract sciences. I do not think this likely, but I think it
could happen. I do not want to make up my mind about
such possibilities, and then shut it down because my aesthetic
sense alone *prefers* what it thinks it sees.

It is, to be sure, hard work to get things right, especially
when they don't turn out to fit exactly the story one hoped
to tell. It is not the duty of the fiction writer to falsify real
facts; he ought instead to be heightening them, making them
more real, not less so. The alternative is to lose all respect
for any aspect of fiction but one's own ego. It is not good
practice for an artist in any field to practise his art the easy
way, and reply afterwards to his critics that since he is a
romantic, he ought to be exempted from the life of the mind.
"Orthography is a discipline of the matter, as well as the
manner"; or, as St. Augustine said repeatedly, the Works are
also the Word.

If the writer nevertheless insists that he wishes only to entertain and that art is the farthest thing from his mind, that
is his privilege—but can't we call the result "fantasy" and
be done with it (as Ballantine did the first books of John
Norman's "Gor" series)? To hitch the word "science" to
work of this kind cannot but be downright offensive to the
scientific imagination—and I am not talking here about Asimov or Hal Clement, but about J. B. S. Haldane and the late
Leo Szilard—and at best it is claiming a cachet to which even
the "hard" science-fiction writer has only the most dubious
claims (because not one science-fiction story in several thou-

sand involves anything closer to science than minor technological innovations). "Science-fantasy" may not yet have become a swearword, but it is certainly a contradiction in terms.

I owe further thanks to Brian Aldiss for having shown up
in the then-current *F&SF* ("A Kind of Artistry," Oct. 1962),
thus giving me an issue at hand in fact as well as in metaphor.
This story is unique in the Aldiss canon even today for a
heavy reliance upon rare and obsolete words, quite reminiscent of Merritt; but except for this failing—obviously an
experiment that no writer with Aldiss' sense of cadence could
find viable—it is a stunning performance. It is set so far in
the future that radical changes in human genetics can be
assumed, and are assumed—and they are all defensible, for
here Aldiss is relying on his audience's knowledge, not its
ignorance. Human behavior has not changed an iota: the
gloomy, tortured, emotionally constricted hero is the willing
victim of an Oedipic relationship with his more-than-wife
which is to be taken as being usual for the dying Earth as a
whole, and beneath this already shocking situation lies a re-
surgent brutishness also present in Greek tragedy, and quite
as explicitly. The hero's final escape into animality—or capture by it—is planted on the second page, and is carried
forward thereafter with a logic so quiet that Aldiss' 'Envoi,'
beautifully inevitable though it is, is as stunning as the last
line of a neck-verse.*

In contrast, let us consider an extended example of how
not to do it, also by a British author: Charles Eric Maine's
Fire Past the Future. This is a somewhat older work; it originally appeared in *Amazing* for December 1958 as "The Big
Count-Down," then as "Count-Down" in the English *New
Worlds* from March 1959 to May 1959; then was published
in hard covers by Hodder and Stoughton in England; and

* Republished in *Best SF Stories of Brian W. Aldiss*, Faber and Faber, London,
1965, which appeared in the U.S. a year later as *But Who Can Replace a Man?*

finally appeared here under the present title as a Ballantine paperback, #360K. This is a pretty good earnings record; and, like the kid in *Peanuts* who jumped into a pile of dead leaves holding a wet lollipop, the reader emerges from the novel with quite a few fragments sticking to his memory. It is, in fact, the only one of the ten books the author had published up to that time for which I can find reason to excuse the publishers; the rest of his work is unrelievedly awful.

As usual, Maine's contempt for science fiction, its readers and its writers is evident in elementary scientific errors, slip-shod dialogue and other forms of inattention. All but one of the eight major characters (the narrative's viewpoint charac-ter) are said to be scientists, but Maine apparently has never met even one. Those in the story are constantly exchanging such remarks as "In science there is always an explanation for the inexplicable," a faith which vanished from the sciences about the time of Einstein's paper "Electrodynamics of Mov-ing Bodies" (1905). Everyone in the book is supposed to be American, but by page eight they are already referring to stew as "M and V." (The hero says he would prefer it iced.)

The science not only includes but depends upon such char-acteristic, long-familiar bloopers as:

(1) " '. . . Space curvature shows the presence of a gravi-tational field. The stronger the field, the greater the curva-ture.' " (Space curvature *is* a gravitational field, and shows the presence of matter.) " 'But if you bend space the other way you create conditions of negative gravity.' " (Uh . . . which way is the other way?)

(2) " '. . . Here on Earth a falling body accelerates at thirty-two feet per second every second, and keeps on accel-erating. If it could keep falling long enough it would eventu-ally attain the speed of light.' " (No material body, under the scholium Maine is appealing to, can attain the speed of light. Furthermore, a body falling to Earth from infinity—which

ought to fit anybody's definition of "long enough"—would arrive with a relative velocity of seven miles per second.)

As the first example shows, Maine is here joining the long list of authors to take a tussle with relativity, without (as the second example shows) even a vague grasp of freshman high school physics. As was wholly predictable, he is finally thrown flat on his back by the Lorentz-FitzGerald Contraction, which despite its apparent simplicity seems to be the Number One deadfall of sloppy or mystical science-fiction writers. I hope that some day such a writer will explain to me why he finds it so easy to accept that a body can have infinite mass, and why he invariably ignores the "zero length" clause that goes with the first impossible condition. However, I am not holding my breath.

But I started out by saying that this novel has some shreds of merit, and it does. Essentially it is a murder story to the model of *And Then There Were None*. Of the eight major characters, all isolated on an atoll for a government-sponsored test of Maine's idiot theory of anti-gravity, six have been killed by the time the test takes place, and the other two are at each other's throats. Since these two are the hero and his beloved, this makes for considerable tension, much of it well handled. There are excellent scenes of suspense, stalking, interpersonal conflicts and violence, and one which is genuinely eerie (plus one which should have been but isn't). The reader has already been told that the hero committed the first murder, and that the heroine has committed the last one, but the other four are entertainingly difficult to account for until Maine is ready to let you in on their mechanics.

"Mechanics" is about all there is to it, however, since it turns out that nobody has been responsible for his own actions and hence the murders are all unmotivated as far as the characters are concerned. The "real" murderer is a *deus ex machina*, whose existence is first deduced by the characters from no evidence at all, and then turns out to match their deductions at every point. In short, sloppiness triumphs over everything else in the end.

And this is the whole of my point. Sloppiness, once embraced, always triumphs; for it is not simply a failure of technique, but a state of mind.

In addition to his other problems, Maine in *Fire Past the Future* has erected for himself a hurdle which is to his credit, at least as an ambition: The book attempts to be a hybrid between science fiction and the detective story. A number of serious science-fiction writers have tried this, Asimov in particular. I think it is a foredoomed exercise, simply because the possibilities for surprise or outright magic in the science-fiction canon are so great that even as scrupulous a writer as Asimov cannot play as fair with the reader as the classical detective story requires; the end result inevitably cannot satisfy the addicts of either specialty. But I cannot fault any man for trying. That is the way an idiom grows—through its mistakes, one of which may eventually turn out not to have been a mistake at all.

The attempt has its further uses for me as a critic, however, because it bears on the question of definition, which I am worrying just as hard near the end of this book as I was at the beginning (probably to nobody's surprise, least of all my own). A hybrid of this kind is very close—perilously, in my judgment—to what Damon Knight has called a "translation." I think Damon's term is poorly chosen, but he defines it aptly by saying that if a story might just as well have taken place in Australia, then it *should* have taken place in Australia.

As it happens, I have to hand an admirable example of just what is meant from the pen of an Australian critic, John Foyster.* He summarizes as follows a story called "The Three Thieves of Japetus," by Mark Reinsberg (from *Imagination*, June 1957):

* *Australian Science Fiction Review*, December 1967, p. 34.

The three thieves lie in wait for a freighter carrying a "valuable cargo." They feign helplessness and are taken aboard by the unsuspecting crew. Then they draw their guns and force the crew out of the spaceship to die. The cargo, it seems, consists of vital supplies for Titan. One of the three must go to deliver an ultimatum. While he is away the others realize that the money will go further between two. When he returns with the news that the money will be sent, and some bottles of whiskey, he is shot. The remaining thieves discover that the dead one had been followed by the Space Police. Having taken a swig of whiskey, they prepare to defend themselves, but realize too late that it is poisoned. They die and exit left.	The three owlhoots lie in wait for a stagecoach carrying a "valuable cargo." They feign thirst and are taken aboard by the unsuspecting stagehands [sic]. Then they draw their sixguns and force the cowpokes from the stage, to die in the desert. The cargo, it seems, consists of rifles for the defenders of Tombstone. One of the three must ride into town to deliver an ultimatum. While he is away the others realize that the money will go further between two. When he returns with the news that the money will be sent, and some bottles of whiskey, he is shot. The remaining owlhoots discover that the dead one had been followed by the Sheriff's Posse. Having taken a swig of whiskey, they prepare to defend themselves, but realize too late that it is poisoned. They die and exit left.

Old owlhoots in our birth-corral will recall that Horace Gold used to run exactly this same kind of parallel-column demonstration on the back cover of his magazine, confined to the presumptive first paragraph of a translation, not the entire plot, under the headline, "You'll Never See It in Galaxy!" The promise was not kept; Gold bought a whole *series* of such stories, the AAA Ace series, from Robert Sheckley, as well as many single samples from other writers. He was not alone, before, then, or since. Foyster's example is chosen from one of the few published stories of an utterly minor writer published in a virtually unread magazine more than ten years ago; but is it then an exercise in archeology (or even paleontology)? Alas, no: witness "—And Devious the Line of Duty," (*ASF*, December 1962) by the constantly mentioned Tom Godwin, a chemically pure translation in that even its original could never have existed (e.g., there may once have been such a place as Australia, but there never was any such place as the Golden West, which involves us at once in two quite different kinds of translations.)

The Never-Never Land exploited by Godwin in this story is called the planet Vesta, which if we took the name seriously would promptly involve us in a confusion with the real, major asteroid called Vesta; but I see no signs that Godwin has ever heard of such a real asteroid.   Only a moment's quite un-critical examination of Godwin's story shows that its real name is Graustark.   Flensing it of its blasters and tree-tigers, we are left with a tale of a beautiful princess who is being forced to marry a slob of a nobleman, in deference to a deathbed promise to her father the king, though in her heart of hearts she loves another.   Along comes a young officer and his cynical, conniving superior, who want to free her from this loveless attachment, the one for love of the princess, the other for love of country.   Alarums, excursions and life-saving exploits.   Exit the young officer in favor of the man the princess really loved all the time.   Curtain, with flowers.

I don't suppose I have to retell an authentic fairy-tale, à la Foyster or Gold, to point the parallels.   In any event, I am much more interested in making the point that most of the stories Damon wanted to call "translations" were like this: not really authentic top-dressings upon possible stories, but only translated Westerns, translated *Saturday Evening Post* stories, or (mostly in *F&SF*) translated soap operas.   They were not about any real places or real people even to start with; they simply adapted various Never-Never Lands and traditions for the purposes of the beanie-and-blaster audience. By the time we have reached this remove, the term "trans-lation" is not only a misnomer, but actively misleading.

The minute one makes this additional distinction, one can also see that all such third-degeneration stories are stories that could not have been sold inside their proper conventions

(Western, soap-opera, etc.) because they are desperately incompetent. They were rescued for print only by the addition of a cupful of Martian sand and the substitution of a robot for the Other Woman.

The Godwin story has no human beings in it, it is bankrupt in invention, and it is in every other way too somnambulistic a piece of story-telling to have been salable *anywhere else* but to a science-fiction magazine (and to the 1962 Hugo winner, at that). I propose a test of this judgment: Let Godwin change the names and trappings, but otherwise repeat the story exactly—after all, self-plagiarism is not a crime—and see how far he gets with it in any other market. Even the internal details will not be new to the ordinary editor of "mundane" fiction. For instance, Godwin's most original notion is a talking dog, who, like Sprague de Camp's talking bear, or World War II's talking Japanese, cannot pronounce the letter "l" and so uses "r" instead. This makes him unintelligible, but mighty cute, at least to any reader under twelve.

I claim no originality for the observation that adapted fairy tales have always been staple fare in science fiction, which is, after all, a sub-section of fantasy. What concerns me is that no other market I know—and I have written for a good many—would sit still for an adaptation as transparent and essentially *un*transformed as this one is. The mere act of removing a cliché to an imaginary planet, on the other hand, still appears to put science-fiction editors and readers alike into second-stage anesthesia. Is *this*, in God's name, what we mean when we try to sell laymen on our wide-ranging imaginations and freedom to say what we wish? No wonder most mainstream critics think us idiots, and intolerably pretentious idiots at that.

In recent years I have been moved to a reluctant admiration for Mack Reynolds—admiration for his rare cosmopolitanism, the bold way in which he tackles touch-me-not political problems and the sense of urgency he obviously feels about them; and reluctant because he is so hasty a writer that his clumsiness is constantly at war with his intentions.

"Speakeasy" in the January 1963 *F&SF* is a case in point. Reynolds has a bill of particulars to offer against conformity. This is what he calls it, but in the story it turns out to be a form of official thought-control, which is something else entirely. (The essence of conformity is self-enforcement, either through timidity or through conviction. Conformity with the force of the law behind it becomes censorship, a very different problem.) The author's first move, then, has been unwittingly to duck the issue he set out to raise.

He has a cute notion, however: that in a society where freedom of expression is forbidden, it will be bootlegged (hence the punning title). I know of no supporting example in the long, sad history of repressive societies, which is why the notion seems to me to be no more than cute. [But there have been recent reports of the circulation of officially unpublishable work in manuscript form in the USSR, which is at least analogous to Reynold's speakeasies.] Its development, in which the in-group circle of the heads of state turns out to be the ultimate speakeasy, is only a standard van Vogtism, as is the ease with which the heads of state decide to make the ignorant, ineffective, stupid, surlily rebellious "hero" into the Lord High Executioner of the whole shebang—preposterous, but a familiar form of preposterousness.

Reynolds is preposterous not only on a grand scale, but all the way down to the bottom. I call your attention to the scene on page 112 of the magazine. Here the hero has been in a scuffle with a Security official who is bigger and more skillful than he is and who consequently bangs him up almost ad libitum. While this fight is going on, the hero manages to get his own hand into his own pocket, and out again, without his bigger and more experienced opponent knocking him galley-west six times over during the maneuver. The purpose of this is to get a drop of some chemical onto the enemy's skin (it has been used before in the story). The enemy passes out; and the hero, winded and groaning with pain, says *aloud*: "Thanks Dad, although I doubt if you ever figured on that instant anesthetic discovery of yours ever being used for this purpose."

This Mutter We Doubt Ever Got Muttered is triply unforgivable, because, as I have already observed parenthetically, Reynolds had an earlier opportunity to explain the instant anesthetic — under much more propitious circumstances — and let it go by; and because the explanation doesn't explain, nor does the fact that the hero's father invented it serve any function in the story. The whole piece is filled with such afterthoughts. Reynolds jimmies his characters into jam after jam by making them do irrational things; then he tells you something about the situation that makes that course of action seem even crazier; and only ten pages later does he come up with the same objection the reader made instantly, and tries to answer it by putting a Band-Aid over it.

For a man who has been in this business as long as Reynolds has, this standard of performance is simply unacceptable — and I do not mean to editors, who are obviously willing to buy it in quantity. It should be unacceptable to Reynolds, for it is obscuring and diluting the things he badly wants to say. His series of African pieces, for instance, carried a burden that richly deserved a place in a mass magazine, such as the *SEP*; nor was there any reason of theme or gadgetry that would have prevented this—only of execution. He is trying to sell us important ideas clothed in the style of Doc Savage and The Shadow—in short, below the level of competent pulp magazine performance. This I think is a shame, but it could be remedied, and let no man say positively that Reynolds is incapable of so doing. After all, the enthusiastically clumsy Harry Harrison of *War With the Robots* turned into the Harry Harrison who wrote *Make Room! Make Room!*, and the spectacle of a Mack Reynolds who paid attention to what he was doing would mark no bigger a transformation.

Many science-fiction writers, in fact, do seem to learn from their own mistakes. Now if they could just stop repeating other people's . . . .

As for you, Atheling, goddammit, you're an incurable idealist.

X. MAKING WAVES:
The Good, the Bad,
the Indifferent [1970]

OUR CONFERENCE TODAY [IN BIRMINGHAM, England] is running under the general title of "Speculative Literature." The use of the word "speculative" to denote science fiction and the fringe areas around it seems to have been begun by Robert A. Heinlein back in 1947; but it has only recently caught on. There seem to be two reasons for this: first, some people are now embarrassed by what they think to be the pulp connotations of "science fiction," and want a name that sounds more respectable, and perhaps more acceptable to the academic community; and second, there is a small but highly vocal group of editors and writers in the field who are innocent of any knowledge of science, and want a label that will cover what they do.

It seems to me that the new term is not much of an improvement. Those who promulgate it seem not to have noticed that all fiction is speculative, and that science fiction differs from other types of fiction only in its subject-matter. Surely a good label ought to tell us what that subject-matter is, as do the terms "historical novel" or "Western story." Nor can we call it "future fiction," since that leaves out a lot of the territory—for example, the parallel-worlds story, or time travel into the past. No, I am afraid that if there is any single subject which dominates this genre, it is science and technology, and that Mr. Gernsback's term is therefore still the best we have. It has a virtue, also, which has gone relatively unnoticed: Its grammatical form, cognate with terms like "detective story," also distinguishes it from a recognizably different class of work, of which *Arrowsmith* and the novels of C. P. Snow are examples. These are not science-fiction novels, but novels of science.

I end, as I started, with this question of terminology because before we undertake to shoot down bad science fiction, we ought to know what kind of animal we are gunning for. I therefore propose to rule out of my consideration any story which does not contain any trace of any science, on the grounds that on the contrary, good science fiction must not only contain some science but depend upon it; as Theodore Sturgeon points out, the story ought to be impossible without it.

A further qualification is also important. It is a matter of fact that science fiction today is one form of commercialized category fiction. Once one examines the implications of this statement, much that is wrong about modern science fiction is instantly explicable, though perhaps no less regrettable. For this fact we owe that same Mr. Gernsback a blow to the chops. Prior to 1926, science fiction could be published anywhere, and was; and it was judged by the same standards as other fiction. Some of the pre-1926 work looks naive to us now, but unredeemably dreadful work almost never got past the editors' desks. Today it does so regularly, because there are magazines with deadlines which cannot appear with blank pages, and there is also a firm and ever-widening audience which will devour any kind of science fiction and rarely reads anything else. This is a situation already quite familiar to us in the field of the detective story. Once Gernsback created a periodical ghetto for science fiction, the gate was opened to the regular publication of bad work; in fact, this became inevitable.

I can easily use myself as a horrible example. Of the first thirteen stories that I sold, all in the very early 1940's, only two had any recognizable shred of merit. The other eleven nevertheless saw print, because there were many magazines then and I came cheap. The fact that I knew absolutely nothing about the craft of fiction, and indeed I didn't even begin to learn until after the war, had no bearing on the situation, which was governed solely by deadlines, money and a whole lot of white space.

Editorial standards rose sharply in that decade, but this did not, of course, abolish the production of execrable work—as anyone can testify who has the misfortune to remember the collaborations of Randall Garrett with Lou Tabakow, Robert Silverberg and Larry Janifer. Under present conditions, such trash is the inevitable and perhaps necessary ooze in which the gems will continue to be embedded.

We must not allow this to put us off, or allow the outsider to use it to put us down. Perhaps some of you saw the item in *The Sunday Times* [London] last January in which a British scientist who apparently had something to do with the *Doctor Who* show was quoted as having decided to go in for science fiction on a bigger scale. He added in the next breath, "Of course most science fiction is utter rot," thus establishing his purity and, I suppose, indirectly proclaiming his intentions to improve us. (Judging by *Doctor Who*, he is not leading from strength.) This is a very familiar attitude; again to quote Ted Sturgeon, "Never before in the history of literature has a field been judged so exclusively by its bad examples."*

I have a counter-ploy which I use on such people which is sometimes effective: I ask them, "How many good novels of any kind have you read lately?" Occasionally, you can trap your opponent into admitting that he hasn't in fact read anything in the past twelve months but *Valley of the Dolls*, or that the only modern science fiction he has ever opened was *The Andromeda Strain*, and then you've got him by the scruff; but you have to know your man fairly well to bring this one off.

In criticism, as in teaching, there is no substitute for knowing the subject-matter thoroughly—and also, knowing as much of the surrounding, larger ground as you can possibly cover. People who read nothing but science fiction and fantasy—the Moskowitz syndrome—are fundamentally non-readers, just as people who read nothing but detective stories are non-readers; their gaping jaws signal not wonder, but the utter absence of any thought or sensation at all. They are easy to spot by their reactions when a fifty-year-old story-telling innovation finally reaches science fiction: They are either utterly bowled over by it and proclaim it the wave of the future, or they find it incomprehensible and demand the return of E. E. Smith, who, unfortunately, is dead.

In other words, the subject-matter of science-fiction *criticism* is not science fiction, but literature as a whole, with particular emphasis upon philosophy and craftsmanship. I stress philosophy not only because science is a branch of it, but because all fiction is influenced by the main currents of thought of its time, and to be unaware of these is like having no windows on the east side of the house; you don't get to see the sun until the day is half over. Craftsmanship should

* From that same seminal speech cast before the Little Monsters.

be an obvious item, but I am perpetually startled by how many science-fiction readers, editors and writers try to get by on intuition instead; as for the critics in science fiction, the only ones whose published work shows any awareness of writing as a craft are Damon Knight and Sour Bill Atheling— and before you conclude that I am blowing my own horn, let me add that it is profoundly *dis*satisfying for a creative writer to find that half the informed technical criticism he can find in his chosen field has been written by himself under a pen name.

This point emphasizes, also, that criticism, like creative writing, is essentially a lonely art quite unrelated to sales figures or annual popularity contests. Colin Wilson, in his first and best book [*The Outsider*], remarked that the plots of Dostoievski novels resemble sofa pillows stuffed with lumps of concrete. God knows what he would have said of the plot, if that's the word I'm groping for, of the typical A. Merritt novel, but it is a lovely image and quite just, no matter what one thinks of Dostoievski's strengths in most other departments; bad construction is bad construction, and the fact that millions of readers have failed to detect it means nothing more than does the fact that millions of people have bought defective automobiles, or believed every word that came out of the mouth of Senator Joe McCarthy.

The awards are equally unreliable guides, and for the same reason. The list of the Hugo winners in the science fiction novel is not quite as depressing as a summary of Pulitzer prizes, but give us an equivalent amount of time and we may well beat the Pulitzer jury by miles. Is there a soul who is now alive who remembers *They'd Rather Be Right*, by Mark Clifton and Frank Riley, which in 1955 drew the second Hugo ever awarded a piece of fiction? Unfortunately, I do, and I wish I didn't. And lest you accuse me of shooting sitting ducks, let me add that of the four Heinlein novels which won Hugos, only one is a work of genuine merit, and one is a borderline case; while one took the award away from Kurt Vonnegut's *The Sirens of Titan*, which was not only the best science-fiction novel of its year, but one of the best ever written. The split 1968 novella award to Philip José Farmer is a plain case of the bowling-over of non-readers by daring innovations taken lock, stock and barrel out of the "Cave of the Winds" chapter of Joyce's *Ulysses*, which first saw print in *The Little Review* in 1919. As for the Nebula awards, some of these can be explained only as the product (in the arithmetical sense) of indefatigable log-rolling and pathological faddism. No matter how fair the balloting, small groups are inherently vulnerable to such pressures, since the winning margin can be tiny. (My 1959 Hugo, I was told, was swung only by a last-minute influx of British votes.)

Why should we expect otherwise? Literature, as Richard Rovere has remarked, is not a horse-race; there are no winners and not even any final posts to pass. I am even prepared to entertain the notion that my own Hugo was undeserved, though if I do not hear cries of "No, no," I shall stomp off the platform in a huff. [Solitary cry of "No, no."] Well, it's a good thing I brought my wife. Literary merit is built into the work regardless of who sees it, or how soon he sees it; there is no absolutely reliable guide but the judgment of time, as Matthew Arnold said. No individual critic has the lifespan to wait time out—observe, for instance, the fluctuating reputations of Chaucer, Shakespeare, Johann Sebastian Bach—and his only recourse is to make himself the master of his subject as best he can, and defend his perceptions of the good, the bad and the indifferent against juries, shifts in taste, ignorance, popularity contests and all other forms of mob action, including other critics who are trying to create or mount bandwagons.

And there is one other defense the critic has, if he has the heart for it. If he does, it will save him a lot of acrimony,

and vastly enlarge his own appreciation of the work he is
criticizing. Unhappily, it is the rarest of all critical attributes,
as well as the most admirable:

He should not be afraid to change his mind.

Entertaining a change of mind appears to be extraordi-
narily difficult for a segment of s-f fandom, for all the fans'
claims to wider mental horizons than the mainstream reader.
As I have noted above, and had earlier at the Pittcon (*The
Issue at Hand*, p. 128), science fiction is now old enough so
that there are now some readers who have been reading it
since childhood and regard it as comfortable and safe—and
do not want it to change. It is for them a sort of pastoral,
in which spacemen take the place of shepherds (apparently
they are opposed to shepherdesses) and space becomes the
meadow of refuge from the more complex affairs of the
world around them.

But of course it *will* change all the same, and in recent
years the change has come to be called the New Wave. This
is now old enough so that it is possible to attempt a characterization of it. It has consisted mainly of the following
elements: (1) Heavy emphasis upon the problems of the
present, such as overpopulation, racism, pollution and the
Vietnam war, sometimes only slightly disguised by s-f trappings; (2) Heavy emphasis upon the manner in which a story
is told, sometimes almost to the exclusion of its matter, and
with an accompanying borrowing of devices old in the mainstream but new to science fiction, such as stream of consciousness, dadaism, typographical tricks, on-stage sex, Yellow
Book horror and naughty words; (3) Loud claims that this
is the direction in which science fiction must go, and all other
forms of practice in the field are fossilized; (4) Some genuinely new and worthy experiments embedded in the mud.

Let's look closer—and try to keep our heads.

Like most movements in the arts (in music there are the

examples of the French Six and the Russian Five), the New Wave in science fiction includes a number of people whose aims and approaches are quite different. Hence at the outset the critic who wants to discuss it is confronted with the problem of just what it is he is talking about; furthermore, each critic may have a separate cast of characters, so I had best start by identifying my own.

The chiefest advocate of the New Wave—or the most vocal, at least up to 1967, when a contender surfaced—was Judith Merril. Though she is the author of a small number of short stories, including one good one and one very well known one (not identical), and two sentimental novels, Miss Merril is mainly an editor and book reviewer whose reputation rests upon a series of annual anthologies of "Best S-F" stories.

These anthologies had an enormous influence on the New Wave, quite apart from Miss Merril's subsequent championing of it. They were originally fairly conventional productions, quite well edited but otherwise distinguished only by the impressiveness of their publisher, Simon and Schuster. The conventionality was in part a by-product of the publisher, in fact. In the early years of the project, Miss Merril was required to submit for each volume many more stories than could actually be used, and the final selection was made in the publisher's office; the rejects ended up as "honorable mentions." To the best of my knowledge, no public acknowledgement of this procedure was ever made; but as Miss Merril's reputation grew and her choices became more idiosyncratic, it led to a break and a search for another publisher which wound up at Delacorte.

The change in emphasis which led to the break may most succinctly be described as an outcome of education. As can be seen in her early fan magazine writings, particularly for the Vanguard Amateur Press Association, Miss Merril at the beginning of her career resembled most other young fans of the day in having read almost nothing but science fiction and fantasy; her knowledge of literature at large was bounded on one side by Walt Whitman and on the other by Thomas Wolfe. Unlike the standard model of such fans, however, her reading widened, at first apparently out of a desire (perhaps the publisher's, rather than her own) to make science fiction look respectable by cramming into the anthologies as many famous names as possible. Whatever the motive, the actual process inevitably involved a whole series of belated literary discoveries in Miss Merril's middle years, and these in turn were reflected in the anthologies; the most recent books in the series have in fact been described as fundamentally auto- biographical by several critics (particularly, Algis Budrys and Brian W. Aldiss).

There is, however, another contributing factor, upon which only Budrys has previously commented and that only glancingly: In the beginning, Miss Merril knew as little about the sciences as she did about the arts, and indeed never has felt comfortable with them. These two traits—belated discovery of mainstream literature, and continuing non- comprehension of the scientific enterprise and spirit—seem to have been catalyzed by a proposal Damon Knight took from Heinlein that science is not absolutely essential to science fiction, and that the genre might equally well be called "speculative" fiction.*

Miss Merril seized this proposal as avidly as though it were a life preserver, and promptly announced (in the 11th anthology, 1966) that henceforth the "S" in the "S-F" of her anthology title meant "speculative." This rubric has since been used to justify the inclusion in the annuals of fantasies, surrealist pastiches, bad verse, comic strips, political satire, pseudo-scientific articles, old jokes, macabre cartoons, how-to-write-it pieces, ancient reprints, perfectly ordinary mainstream stories, and in fact anything at all that Miss Merril discovered that she liked.

* *In Search of Wonder*, revised edition, pp. 1, 5; *The Issue at Hand*, p. 33.

Except for the implicit deception involved, such catholicity is very far from being a bad thing. It is certainly more broadening for all concerned than trying to become the Greatest Living Authority on science fiction alone, which is about as rewarding as being the Greatest Living Authority upon the fishes of Penobscot Bay. Miss Merril was tempted, as her 1962 dog-in-the-manger attack upon Kingsley Amis painfully revealed; but it is entirely to her credit that she did not fall.

The choice, furthermore, paid off. There turned out to be a large number of writers and fans waiting in the wings who were as uncomfortable with, or actively distrustful of, the sciences as Miss Merril, and for whom the "speculative" formulation was equally liberating and self-justifying. They had always been there (e.g., Bradbury) but they had never before had a critical banner. Perhaps the Heinlein-Knight pioneer proposal had been too tentative for them; Miss Merril's had the all-out fervor of a mystical experience.

The proclamation also was issued at a peculiarly favorable time. Though modern science fiction had earlier spawned some highly literate and/or self-consciously experimental writers like Theodore Sturgeon and Philip José Farmer, it happened that there was a high concentration of them in the field in this particular period. Accidentally, most of them were English, but even that accident proved timely and fruitful.

At the head of this group must stand J. G. Ballard; though he is a totally solitary man impossible to imagine in a group, impossible to imitate, and not the best writer of the New Wave, he was already well known to the science fiction audience as an explosively original writer, and even today most arguments about the meaning and value of the movement whirl around his head—a situation exacerbated by the fact that, as a reviewer for a newspaper, he has taken the position that he has made all of his predecessors and most of his contemporaries old hat.

Ballard is the author of four book-length novels to date, all of which belong to that peculiar British type which might be dubbed the one-lung catastrophe, pioneered by, of all people, Conan Doyle. In stories of this type, the world is drowned, parched, hit by a comet, smothered by volcanic gas, sterilized by the Van Allen belts, or otherwise revisited by some version of Noah's Fludde; and the rest of the story deals either with the Ark or with Adam and Eve. (In Ballard's versions, everybody gives up and nobody survives.) Ballard is not especially good at this kind of thing, partly because of the almost pathological helplessness of his characters, and partly because his rationales either make little sense or are not revealed at all (though it must be admitted that *The Crystal World* is lovely nevertheless). His real radicalism shows in his short stories.

For about ten years, Ballard has been engaged in putting together a myth. Those short stories which do not belong to an identifiable, conventional series—such as the Vermilion Sands stories—are pieces of a mosaic, the central subject of which is not yet visible, rather as though a painter were to go about making a portrait by filling in the background in minute detail and leaving a silhouetted hole where the sitter should be. The nature of this attempt has been somewhat masked by the fact that the minor characters—of which there are not very many—sometimes appear in the stories under different names; but there can be little doubt that these fragments (which are the Ballard works which most exacerbate his detractors) are going somewhere, by the most unusual method of trying to surround it, or work into it from the edges of the frame. The difficulty of seeing it whole is further compounded by the equally odd choices Ballard makes of narrative method — for example, presenting one fragment in the form of the notes of a psychotic, another as articles excerpted from some mad encyclopedia. He calls these pieces "condensed novels," and has published them as a collection, but clearly the enterprise is far from being finished.

The outcome may be a failure, or it may be a seminal masterpiece. Nobody at this point in the attempt's history could possibly predict which; the plain, blunt fact is that we do not yet know what it is Ballard is talking about (and, of course, there is always the possibility that he doesn't either; we shall just have to wait and see). That Ballard is not very good as a conventional science-fiction novelist is quite beside the point, since Ballard's mosaic myth is not a conventional novel and has no antecedents. (Confronted by anything out of the ordinary in science fiction, even friendly critics like Miss Merril are all too ready to compare it to something they call *Finnegan's Wake*; but in Ballard's case, as in all the others but one, there turns out to be no such relationship. Michael Moorcock has said that Ballard is the originator of his form; I think this is true.) Ballard has a most imperfect grasp of the sciences—he uses "quasars" like authors of the 1920's used "radium," as a magic word—and his discipline is dubious, but he also has a great deal of raw creativity and is a poet; and these, I take it, are the four qualities which characterize almost all the New Wave writers.

Almost; but I will immediately have to except Brian W. Aldiss, who is not ignorant of the sciences (though he sometimes scamps them) and is perhaps the most thorough, disciplined professional ever to concentrate his gifts upon science fiction. As a man who loves the English language with a profound and contagious passion, and knows it far too well to be showy about it, Aldiss was from the beginning almost in himself a New Wave in science fiction, and almost for that reason alone got lumped in with the group (and seems to be much in sympathy with it); but he differs from almost everybody else in it not only by being almost always in control of what he writes, but also by being convinced of the *desirability* of being in control. In consequence, he is virtually the only

New Wave writer who never offers aborted experiments in the disguise of finished work. It sometimes seems, indeed, that only Aldiss' receptivity, and his willingness to try any drink once, tie him to the New Wave at all; but as a poet and an experimentalist he belongs with them, however more easy to take his professionalism makes his work for the ordinary reader. For example, his *Report on Probability A*, though it is the first attempt to adapt the French anti-novel to a science-fictional end, and does not succeed at it, is so cunningly carpentered that even its failure is definitive; while *Barefoot in the Head*, which actually does derive heavily and directly from late Joyce, brings JJ's "Eurish" as close to accessibility by the ordinary reader as it is ever likely to come. (More about *Barefoot* later.)

John Brunner is also a poet and an experimentalist with a thoroughly professional approach, and has appeared in *New Worlds*; two of his books, including the dinosaurian, Hugo-winning *Stand on Zanzibar*, confessedly borrow techniques wholesale from Dos Passos, for example. Yet I find myself hesitating to think of him as a New Wave writer, for reasons so unclear to me that they are probably invalid. Always staggeringly prolific, Brunner has in his past a good many completely conventional s-f books (as has Aldiss, although on a considerably smaller scale) and even his experimental work shows many of the conventional stigmata, such as a predominance of wheeler-dealer characters and the imposition of mechanically pat endings. He is, however, clearly a perfectionist by nature and one may confidently expect these blemishes to disappear sooner or later; in the meantime, so much that was conventional has already been eliminated from his work that to rule him out of the New Wave would in logic force one to conclude that there was no such thing as a New Wave at all.

Another important figure is Michael Moorcock, for whose reconstructed magazine *New Worlds* Aldiss finagled an Arts

Council grant of £1,800 ($4,320), and whom Aldiss has called an editorial genius. This judgment is perhaps a little excessive. Rather like Miss Merril, Moorcock was a fan who until assuming this editorship had exhibited no signs of talent for writing (his major productions were the worst kind of sword-and-sorcery hackwork, carefully hidden under a pen name until it was revealed by one of *his* editors, Ted White). When he was put in charge of *New Worlds*, he turned it physically into a semi-slick, thin magazine resembling the *New Scientist* (a British version of *Scientific American*, but much less expensively produced), and engaged for it the worst distributor in England (in three weeks of looking for the current issue all over London in 1967, I found only one copy, in Paddington Station, and Britain's two major newsstand chains, Smith and Menzies, stock and display the magazine even today both seldom and erratically). He filled a large part of his limited space with non-illustrative art-work, mostly surrealism and collages, plus art-nouveau and psychedelic designs, together with articles about these pic-tures written in a pastiche of the mindless jargon of the American *Art News*.

The purpose of this format, as was (perhaps apocryphally) explained in 1969 by an interim editor, James Sallis, was to provide a home for a wide range of manifestations of the modern age, including but not confined to science fiction. Nevertheless, quite a lot of science fiction did appear there, including *Report on Probability A*, much of *Barefoot in the Head* and all of Disch's *Camp Concentration*, and in making up a first selection of such pieces for a book, Moorcock led from strength and chose well. The non-science fiction in the magazine has been predictably obsessed with drugs and the Vietnam war, and Moorcock's own chief fictional contribu-tion has been an interminable series about an imitation James Bond named Jerry Cornelius. A Moorcock story in *New Worlds*, called "Behold the Man," later became a novel which won a Nebula in 1968.

Harlan Ellison is not only the most audible but possibly the most gifted of the American members of the New Wave. When he first hove into sight in 1956, spinning around lamp-posts and bragging of imaginary adventures and achievements, I thought him all noise and no talent, and told him so. In the succeeding decade he proved me dead wrong about this, and very few acts as a writer have given me so much pleasure as acknowledging this (in a 1967 book dedication). Personally, Harlan can be very engaging, but he can also be the most annoying man in the world; this blinded me. He is in fact a born writer, almost entirely without taste or control but with so much fire, originality and drive, as well as compassion, that he makes the conventional virtues of the artist seem almost irrelevant; his work strongly resembles that of Louis-Ferdinand Céline (of whom he has probably never heard*), even to its black, wild humor. (He can also be a superb technician if somebody else is in a position to force him to be, as a television script of his I have seen attests; but he is almost the embodiment of the old saying that it takes two men to make a masterpiece—one man to hold the brush, and one man standing behind the first with a hammer to hit him on the head with when it's finished.) He is as ignorant of the sciences as a polliwog, and just as happy in that state; what he writes are fantasies of violence and love, every one an experiment and seldom the same experiment twice. Of course these do not always work, but when they do the re-sults are explosive. (He is both a Hugo and a Nebula winner.)

His grandest experiment to date is *Dangerous Visions* and its successor. Without throwing around terms like "editorial genius," it might be noted that selling, organizing, collecting and promoting this collection of 33 original stories (xxix + 520 pp.), much of the advance money for which came out of Ellison's own pocket, required editorial control and per-

* I was wrong about this, too.

sistence of no mean order; and as for editorial acumen, the prizes collected by the stories included, and the sales record of the collection, do not suggest that Ellison did not know what he was doing. The sequel, *Again, Dangerous Visions*, hasn't appeared at this writing, but as of January 1970 the fiction content alone (as will be noted below, the editorial gristle in an Ellison anthology tends to be extensive) had reached 436,000 words, or seven times the length of the average novel.

In one of the introductions to the parent volume, Ellison says: "By the very nature of what they write, many authors were excluded because they had said what they had to say years ago. Others found that they had nothing controversial or daring to contribute. Some expressed lack of interest in the project." Still another reason for non-inclusion is suggested by Poul Anderson, who *is* represented but who "insists [his story] is not 'dangerous' and could have sold to any magazine." Ellison ducks this point by invoking now impossible outlets for it (*McCall's* and *Boys' Life*), but the fact remains that Anderson is right—and furthermore, there is *no* story in this collection that would have been rejected *for thematic reasons* by any of the current science-fiction magazines. At least some unrepresented writers probably doubted, with reason, that anything is inherently unpublishable in these Grove Press days simply because of its subject-matter.

But it should be noted that there is a substantial hole in this argument, and the truly revolutionary nature of *Dangerous Visions* is concealed in it. While almost any one of these stories *could* have appeared in, say, *If* or *Analog*, it would have been surrounded there by more conventional pieces. This book consists of *nothing but* experiments. As such, it is indeed a monument, and will be a gold mine of new techniques and influences for writers for many years to come. It may also, eventually, drastically change readers' tastes, and perhaps even the whole direction of the field.

It is hard reading on several different counts. One of its problems, which could have been avoided, is that it is overloaded with apparatus: there are three prefaces, and each story is both preceded by an introduction in which the editor explains the author, and followed by an afterword in which the author explains himself. This is too much, and tends to suggest an air of distrust in the whole project which is heightened by the shrilly aggressive tone of much of the editor's copy. Good wine needs no bush.

Another minor drawback, quite *un*avoidable, is that in a collection in which all the stories are determinedly peculiar, none of them shines as brightly as it might have, had it been embedded in more conventional work. They tend to pull each other's teeth. However, the reader can remedy this for himself, simply by sampling, and giving each individual story ample time to sink in.

Finally—and again, unavoidably—well more than half of these experimental stories are failures, as any reasonable man would expect of any body of experiments. Some are simply assemblages of typographical tricks; some are wearisomely portentous; some are one-punchers which are not as shocking as they were intended to be, or are even quite predictable; some are incoherent, and a few exhibit a distressingly small acquaintance with the English language, or even a positive distaste for it. The Farmer story, the longest in the book, shows almost all of these faults at once (and, it is the story mentioned in the opening of this chapter which split the Hugo award for the novella for 1968).

Except for the excessive editorial matter (some of which, to be sure, is delightfully witty), these drawbacks are intrinsic to the nature of the project, and nobody should allow himself to be put off by them. There has never been a collection like this before, and both Ellison and Doubleday deserve well of us for it.

Two American members of the group whom Ellison has published, and both of whom are both Nebula and Hugo winners, are Roger Zelazny and Samuel R. Delany, whose work resembles Ellison's in many respects—particularly in exuberance, efflorescent vocabulary, and very little control over either internal detail or major form; however, they resemble each other more than they do anyone else, as both seem well aware.* Though Zelazny made his first mark as a short-story writer and Delany his as a novelist, both are primarily retellers of myths in science-fictional terms, with complex cross-references to literary systems derived from myth which show a scholar's bent for which Ellison lacks patience, and probably inclination too. Of the two, I find Delany harder to read, because his imagery is so constantly to the fore, and so consistently foggy, that I often suspect that he himself does not know what he means by it—and his explanations (in the fan press and on the academic lecture platform) seem to fog the matter still further. Here I am very much out of step. His novel *Babel 17* won a Nebula as the best of 1966, but I thought it pretty close to being the worst, and when his *The Einstein Intersection* won the same award in 1968, I stepped quietly out into the kitchen and bit my cat. That Delany has drive, insight, and a certain music I cannot doubt, but neither his clotted style nor his zigzag way of organizing a story strike me as being much better than self-indulgent and misdirected. If I am right about this—and my experience with Ellison suggests that I am more than likely to be wrong about it—Delany's early popularity, laid on

---

* There can be few science-fiction fans who have not met both men, but for those who have not, the assonance of their names is a complete accident and neither is a pen name for the other. Delany is a merry and handsome young Negro who travels in hippie dress and has educated himself as a composer as well as a writer; Zelazny is a courtly young white of Polish ancestry who looks like the business end of a hatchet and works for the Social Security Administration in Baltimore (as of 1969). The similarities in their approaches to science fiction would pose a major puzzle to any purely biographical critic.

well before he was either in control or was convinced of the necessity of being in control of his manner or his matter, may well turn out to be destructive. He would not be the first writer whom immoderate early praise (though every writer longs for it) put out of business, at least for a damagingly long period; see my remarks on Sturgeon.

But there is hope for the Nebula voters yet. In 1969 they gave a Nebula to Richard Wilson, whose high, clean, and heart-breakingly precise narrative prose I recommended as a corrective to Chip Delany on our first meeting in 1965, much to the embarrassment of both men. I am still dead sure that Wilson's way, which would be classified as "uptight" by Delany's admirers, is the better of the two, and likely to last the longer.

I am somewhat more in sympathy with Zelazny's work, mainly because he pays closer attention to the sciences (though intermittently, like Aldiss) and his attitude toward language is not so anarchistic (quite unlike Aldiss, who started as a formalist and is now a terrorist). But both Delany and Zelazny share with each other first of all, and secondarily with all the major New Wave writers except John Brunner, a dangerously ill-considered attitude (it is now very close to being a fad). There is no standard critical term for it, since it appears to be obsessive only in modern science fiction, though it was around before. I have therefore invented my own term: *mytholatry*. It is a term which I may never use again, but just in case I must, I offer an extended definition, with clay feetnote. The definitive example is *Creatures of Light and Darkness*, by Roger Zelazny.

The publication of Joyce's *Ulysses* in 1924 prompted T. S. Eliot to suggest that for the modern novel in general, myth might prove an acceptable replacement for poetic structure or plot. In our field, we saw a lot of use of myth in the *Unknown* era—Pratt/de Camp come to mind at once—but these stories were games. It has remained for the New Wave writers, some 45 years later, to catch up with Eliot's proposal. Lately we have seen Chip Delany (to whom the present novel is dedicated, not, I think, "Just Because") and Michael Moorcock take on the Christ myth; Zelazny in *Lord of Light* adopted Hindu mythology, and Greek in *This Immortal*; and Emil Petaja has been hashing his way through the Finnish *Kalevala* . . . all in dead earnest.

Zelazny's *Creatures of Light and Darkness* tries to turn Egyptian mythology into a serious science-fiction novel. Despite some good passages, I think it is a flat failure.

It is a failure in conception. No excuse at all is offered for its primary assumption that the Egyptian gods were real creatures with real power to control the universe of experience, for the lack of any evidence for this in thousands of years of real Egyptian writings about them, or for their survival as creatures of power into the very far future. The notion is utterly arbitrary; a cute notion is all it is.

It is ignorant and inconsistent. The personifications of the gods in Zelazny's hands are undignified, stupid, uncharacteristic and anti-historical. Creatures from other mythologies (e.g., the Norns, Cerberus, the Minotaur) are shoved in at random, as are several which are apparently Zelazny inventions. One of the inventions is an ineducable immortal called the Steel General with a fix on lost causes, who owns a mechanical horse which dances senselessly up and down and pulverizes the landscape whenever his master gets into a fight.

Stylistically, it is a hash. Some parts are evocative in the authentic and unique Zelazny manner, but he cannot sustain the tone; the gods call each other "Dad," and a speech that starts out with thee's and thou's winds up with "ambulance-chaser"; a 411-word sentence describing a dead city, intended to be hypnotic, is killed before it starts by the arch instruction, "Color it dust." There are moments of authentic comedy, such as the tentative prayers of Madrak ("Thank you, Dad") to Whomever may or may not be listening, but

most of the putative humor is at the Batman level and seems
just as dated.

Moreover, this is another of those recently multiplying
novels of apparatus, told in bits and scraps, zigzagging among
viewpoints and tenses, and dropping into quotations or verse
for no reason beyond an apparent desire to seem experimental or impressive. The book ends in dramatic form—
that is, as a section from a play—with a scene which absolutely demands straightforward, standard narrative and for
which the playscript is the worst possible choice.

Beyond these blemishes, there is an important theoretical
misconception here. As Darko Suvin has noted, the displace-
ments from the world of experience involved in myth attempt
to explain that world in terms of eternal forces which are
changeless; the attempt is antithetical to the suppositions
of science fiction, which center around the potentialities of
continuous change. Once one invokes such great names as
Anubis, Osiris and Thoth, one willy-nilly also invokes the
whole complex of associations which goes with them, the
static assumptions of a fixed cosmos about which everything
important is already known. You are writing an allegory
whether you want to or not, and if you don't even realize
that this is the problem, the end product is bound to ring
false.

This is the third time Zelazny has fallen into this trap, and
this time around it seems to have put his self-critical sense
completely to sleep. One more like this, and the late Leroy
Tanner will have justified his existence after all.

There is, however, a way out of the trap, entirely viable
for science fiction and mostly lacking—though not entirely
devoid of—the dangers of producing what is chiefly a tricksy
repainting of a stalled machine. This is the difficult path of
creating one's own myth, or showing one in the process of
formation. Here no specific historical instance needs to be
aped; after all, the general process is shown clearly in Frazer's

The Golden Bough (Graves' *The White Goddess* had better be avoided unless the writer is knowledgeable enough to use it highly selectively), and it has the advantage of *being* a process, with an open end, rather than a rigidly boxed universe tied with the ribbons of some particular sect.

Aldiss has done this in *Barefoot in the Head*, and the result is so spectacular — and so complex — that it merits close study.

In the *Sunday Times* [London] early in 1970, a very well-known reviewer awarded almost awed praise to a novel which —as his highly detailed plot summary made clear—was only another worn retread of the post-World War III barbarism story. The present text is also set in a post-World War III barbarism, although a mint-original one; and on the immediately preceding Sunday, a *Times* reviewer unknown to me gave it about three paragraphs so uninformative about the book and so abusive in tone as to suggest some sort of personal vendetta.

If jealousy or enmity is not the answer, then what did make the difference? for clearly the Aldiss—to a disinterested eye, however unfriendly—could not possibly be all that bad, and its successor in the same pages merited virtually no attention, let alone praise. One reason might be found in the fact that the blurb on the jacket of *Barefoot* twice mentions science fiction, while the other book was published "straight"; many readers, and almost all publishers, still have compartments in their heads stuffed with broken dolls, like the striking Erró jacket illustration for Aldiss' novel.

But I think the difficulty reaches more deeply than that. Aldiss' war, like that in Franz Werfel's *Star of the Unborn*, was fought with psychedelic agents (now a much more likely proposition than it was in Werfel's day) and in consequence almost everyone in the novel is mad—and the language reflects this. They are the "new autorace, born and bred on motorways; on these great one-dimensional roads rolling they mobius-stripped themselves naked to all sensation, beaded, bearded, belted, busted, bepileptic, tearing across the synthetic twen-cen landskip, seaming all the way across Urp, Aish, Chine, leaving them under their reefer-smoke, to the Archangels, godding it across the skidways in creasingack selleration bitch you'm in us all in catagusts of living."

It is not all like this, but there are enough such passages to baffle—and thereby give offense—to the lazy. Clearly the kind of mind that greeted the denser chapters of *Ulysses*, and all of *Finnegans Wake*, with snarls of ignorant scorn is with us yet.

Although *Barefoot* includes one highly explicit bow to *Ulysses* (a hideously effective pun on page 93, "Agenbite of Auschwitz") and resembles it in both structure and narrative (though only in the most fundamental sense in each case), its texture is much more like that of *FW*, even to the echoing of some of *FW*'s most easily recognizable mannerisms (puns that cross over word breaks, chains of long words ending in "-ation," catalogue sentences) and its unique grammar (which, to the best of my knowledge, no other imitator has ever even recognized, let alone captured). Like *Ulysses*, it includes many of the popular songs of its time (in this case, of course, the future); like *FW*, it also includes original verse (some of it the "visual chiromancy," or magic-square arrangement of words so that pictures are also formed, which so fascinated the American scholastic realist, Charles Peirce of Milford; some of it concrete poetry, consisting of repeated letters, or sometimes syllables of words, in what are supposed to be significant arrangements—happily, Aldiss' samples make surface sense, which is rare in this kind of thing).

Okay. It has been observed before by friends of the *New Worlds* school—not often by its enemies, who seldom seem to have read anything but old science fiction—that the techniques it has been exploiting are all thirty to fifty years old: dada, surrealism, vorticism, Dos Passos, and now late Joyce.

The only new aspect of all this is the application of these techniques to science fiction. Though I have expressed in print my disturbance that a genre focussed on Tomorrow should become so fascinated by the idioms and fads of Yesterday, John Brunner has correctly reminded me that Yesterday is just as much a part of the Past as are such techniques as the sonnet. Under this rubric I have no more right to judge a writer harshly for imitating Dos Passos than I would for his faithfully following Fowler's *English Usage*. What counts is: (a) How appropriate is the device in the individual example at hand, and (b) how well assimilated is it, ditto?

Obviously, the smashed and reassembled fragments of language ("the abnihilization of the etym") Joyce invented to tell a dream are equally appropriate for the conveying of the thoughts of madmen bombed (both literally and in the slang sense) "back into the Stone Age" with shattered memories of their old cultures still sticking to them. I am less sanguine about the problem of assimilation. Certainly Aldiss has come closer to making the language of *FW* his own than has anybody but Anthony Burgess; but unlike Burgess' similar passages, Aldiss' are often more Joyce than they are Aldiss, to no visible purpose. Take, for example, the above-mentioned chains of long words ending in "-ation." In *FW*, these chains invariably announce the pub-keeper hero's twelve customers, who in the dream are also the jurymen who are to pass upon his shadowy crimes, and also Joyce's pompously hostile critics; the device is therefore both funny and functional. I can find no such function for it in *Barefoot*, and though echolalia is indeed one of the symptoms of a toppling mind, the borrowing is what strikes the eye first, sending me, at least, on a vain search for Joyce's twelve Doyles. (Or does Brian mean to suggest that Charteris' disciples are analogous figures? An allusion that subtle would be hard to find outside *FW*, too.)

The question may be a relatively minor one, but it further

raises a critical problem which *Barefoot* also shares with *FW*. In the Joyce novel, though it includes chapters told from several different points of view, all these seem to be filtered through the unconscious mind of the dreaming pub-keeper —but there is a fairly substantial section toward the end where he appears to be awake and observed from the outside, though the dream *language* continues. Is it now Joyce's dream? Is it *all* Joyce's dream? Similarly, *Barefoot* shifts viewpoints fairly frequently; but although the language does show that some of the characters are less stoned than others, or stoned in different ways, they all seem to share the same *specific* culture, including details of education. (For the most obvious example, they all have to have read *FW*.) The only way around this is to assume that the language is the author's throughout, and that while the characters are thinking these thoughts and making these speeches, they are not doing so in this way . . . Melville's illiterate sailors spouting high Elizabethan blank verse; Joyce's lower-middle-class barman dreaming in a mixture of thirty languages, including classical Greek and Sanskrit. It's a convention the reader simply must accept for the sake of its poetic effectiveness; should he stop to examine its implications, as though this were a realistic novel, the whole structure will come apart in his hands.

It is somewhat easier to accept the novel's philosophical underpinning. As *FW* leans on Vico and Bruno, so *Barefoot* leans on Ouspenski and Gurdjieff, whom even the walk-ons seem to have read. As mystics go, Ouspenski was a remarkably rational and certainly difficult thinker and it is impossible to imagine a world of acid-heads following him for more than three pages; but his teacher was the more usual kind of nut, a shell of impressive phrases connected any old which way and completely hollow inside, the perfect guru for the world Aldiss describes.

I think I have said enough to show that *Barefoot in the Head* is a long way indeed from being any sort of naturalistic novel, conventional or otherwise. It is a poetic construct, highly artificial, allusive, multi-levelled, symbolic; and built around the skeleton of a convention, the post-Bomb science-fiction novel. (*Gernsbacks Wake?* Oh God.) It is also very difficult to read, unless you actively enjoy an almost continuous stream of puns and portmanteau words; if you do, you will find wit, gusto, and some genuine poetry (I except the imitation pop stuff, whose pretentious emptiness Aldiss has captured all too faithfully) in *Barefoot* . . . and, as an incidental dividend, you will have been nicely trained to take on *FW* itself.

Beneath all the wordplay, and quite frequently on top of it, is a rather simple, straightforward story. Its hero, like the central figures of most recent Aldiss, is a lonely man on a physical odyssey which is also a search for himself, crippled by being ninety percent a product of the madness of his time, and surrounded or assaulted by figures who are totally immersed in and victimised by it. He is a Serb whose *Drang nach Albion* has led him to adopt a literary English name, Colin Charteris, after Leslie Charteris, author of the Saint; and in the Midlands takes over a messiah racket from a fading guru, killing his manager in a semi-accident and also taking over the manager's wife. He is highly successful at the racket, which doesn't entirely surprise him, for from the beginning of the novel he has felt that he has had a new insight into reality, though it remains uncaptured. He leads a motorcade into Europe which ends in a multi-car smashup which, in turn, is restaged as part of a documentary film being made about him; and in an immense premiere in which the film is *not* shown but Brussels is burned down instead, he becomes briefly convinced of his own divinity; and by the end, having become unconvinced, he is en route to becoming a sort of divinity after all, that is, a myth.

Even after allowing for the fact that this plot summary has left out all but one of the important secondary characters,

it is no better an account of the book than would be a summary of *Othello* which told you the play is about a Negro
who murdered his white wife because she had lost her hand-
kerchief. The story could have come from any hand; some
elements of the treatment are distinctly second-hand; but the
whole is unique, moving and almost completely successful.

Be warned, however, that it demands study. Any work of
art, of course, requires study for its understanding; but *Barefoot in the Head* belongs to the more specialized category of
works which without study are incomprehensible even on the
surface. It does begin in a fairly straightforward prose, and
leads only gradually into the multi-level language, but the
farther reaches are complex indeed. Nevertheless, do persist;
the rewards are considerable.

One of them is that this novel, unlike most modern science
fiction, can be mined; it is not simply a diagram or a Tale,
but a world, with rich veins beneath the surface. Among
these is the biological hypothesis that modern man is stuck
with equipment (particularly mental equipment) which served
well enough in the Neolithic Age but is of increasingly less
use as man's world multiplies in complexity. Aldiss never
once says this directly, but instead makes it active in the
fiction: the characters find themselves trapped in a series of
repetitive actual and spiritual experiences, and thanks to the
dazzlement created by the language, neither they nor the
reader can ever be sure that a given event really is a repetition,
or instead a totally new happening being thought about in an
inadequate, inappropriate old way.

Here Aldiss departs decisively from Joyce, for in *FW* the
Viconian cyclical view of history is intended to be taken as a
fact of nature: history does repeat itself, endlessly, in various
guises, and therefore it is appropriate to tell the story of
one such cycle as if it were all of them happening together.
Aldiss, on the other hand, has distorted Ouspenski's mystical
experience of "the eternal return" to a completely subjective

end; history may not in fact repeat itself, but we are going to go on, suicidally, thinking and behaving as if it did.

Almost every aspect of the book, large and small, reinforces and enriches this view of what H. G. Wells, in his last book, called "mind at the end of its tether." The epigraph from General LeMay, and the title of the novel itself, sound the first warnings. The crux of the novel is Charteris' realisation that he has allowed himself to be kidded into sainthood, and the next step is probably crucifixion. He breaks away from his escalating success to seek a new pattern, but since he's stuck with the old equipment, the best he can do is to stop seeking patterns at all, to retreat into ambiguity. He cannot, of course, have it both ways. In a reflective passage, we are told that Charteris was originally named Dušan (a Serbian emperor who fell while he was on his way to conquer Byzantium). By rejecting him and his name, Charteris has committed the repetitive event of not winning himself glory before the story even begins. Angeline, the only loving character, is what that idiot Dr. Edmund Bergler would have called a psychic masochist: she repeatedly, helplessly falls in in love with suicidal false messiahs. By the time Charteris is in love with her, she is out of love (and patience) with him, and he in turn hasn't the equipment to tell her he loves her, he has literally forgotten both the fact itself and how to say it. The repetitive car crash sequences are the product of stone-age brains unable to cope with modern speeds, and in addition are symbolic of the awful speeding up of all events as the book proceeds. The very town of Dover, where an important part of the action takes place, is in living fact just as repetitive an experience as Aldiss paints it as being. People who should be acting remain mired instead in nostalgia (e.g., for Glenn Miller, a childhood memory for some of the characters, a pseudo-memory for the others) or Wordsworthian nature mysticism. Even the imagery is repetitive.

Some of this technique was foreshadowed in *Report on*

Probability A, but *Barefoot* is not an anti-novel; it is evolutionary. Although the hippies who are its people (none of them hippies by their own choice, but the parallels are clear) are incapable of building any new order, the artist can; that is, he can take a situation which is inexorably emptying itself of all meaning, and by re-ordering it, create a structure which in itself has meaning. That is what Aldiss has done.

I should note, finally, that some of these insights came to me from the author directly, not filtered through the book. Ordinarily I would regard this as cheating—after all, how many potential readers could have such an advantage?—but here it is primarily another measure of the novel's complexity. I have been reading the book for less than a year; all these levels of meaning and technique are indubitably there, but I cannot even begin to guess how long it would have taken me to see them all, by myself. I have been reading *FW* since 1939, as well as the immense critical apparatus that continues to build around it, and may now understand perhaps ten percent of it; *Barefoot* is not so formidable, but were it not at least comparable, I shouldn't have raised the issue at all.

It should now be easy to see—at least as easy as it was to predict—that the New Wave has from the beginning been in the process of pulling itself apart. Each of these writers and editors is going in a different and unique direction. One important figure whom I have not discussed, Thomas M. Disch, appears to be headed out of science fiction altogether, insofar as one can judge by his published remarks about "children's literature" and "greener pastures," and the fact that he withdrew his novel *Camp Concentration* from the 1969 Nebula competition. Aldiss is now in an ideal position to do this, too, for he has just published a mainstream novel (*The Hand-Reared Boy*) which was an instant best-seller in Britain, and it is announced as the first volume of a tetralogy; however, at the Birmingham conference referred to at the beginning of this chapter, he reported that he has another science-fiction novel cooking. At the 1969 convention of the British Science Fiction Association at Oxford, Miss Merril announced formally that she was leaving science fiction; but I am inclined to suspect that she did so in about the same spirit that Richard Nixon left politics after his California defeat—and Mr. Nixon had his law practice to fall back upon while he was catching his breath, while science fiction is the only subject Miss Merril knows anything at all about.

That this disintegrative process has reached an advanced stage was visible at the 1970 BSFA Convention, where it was noisily evident that there was nothing formally left of any New Wave group but a dying magazine and a tiny group of drunks and hangers-on, bent chiefly on calling attention to themselves by disrupting the proceedings. It may also be seen in the 1970 Nebula voting, for while both Ellison and Delany won prizes, Norman Spinrad's novel *Bug Jack Barron*, which was aggressively and second-handedly trendy in all the ways that *New Worlds* (where it first appeared) holds dear, did not.

The major figures of the New Wave have quite outgrown the need for such a group, if indeed they ever did need it for moral support or anything else; writers of substance learn early that they have to be their own moral support. Nevertheless, it was a lively old thing while it lasted, filling the local air with shrieks, boasts, counter-crusades, slander, flying glassware, wet firecrackers, propaganda, dead horses, sitting ducks, non-issues, straw men, tin gods, and millions of words of unreadable prose. It also fertilized the production of a surprisingly large number of works of genuine merit, plus a lot of experimentation which even at its worst jarred many people into rethinking their critical stances.

Willy-nilly, we have had a revolution, and it cannot be undone. In retrospect, I can even manage to be grateful for it—a critical stance which might be defined as crockery recollected in tranquility.

Index